PSALMS
73–150

Text copyright © Donald Coggan 1999

The author asserts the moral right
to be identified as the author of this work

Published by
The Bible Reading Fellowship
Sandy Lane West, Oxford, England
ISBN 1 84101 065 0

First edition 1999
10 9 8 7 6 5 4 3 2 1 0

Acknowledgments
Unless otherwise stated, scripture quotations are taken from
The Revised English Bible © Oxford University Press and
Cambridge University Press, 1989.
Extracts from the Authorized Version of the Bible (The King
James Bible), the rights in which are vested in the Crown, are
reproduced by permission of the Crown's Patentee, Cambridge
University Press.
Extracts from *The Alternative Service Book 1980* are copyright ©
The Archbishops' Council and are reproduced by permission.
Material from *Celebrating Common Prayer* (Mowbray), © The
Society of Saint Francis 1992, is used with permission.
Extract from 'I lift my eyes' © Timothy Dudley-Smith, used by
permission.
Extracts from *By Stony Paths* and *Towards the City* © Jim Cotter,
used by permission.
'Doxology' from *Poems of the Western Highlanders* by G.R.D.
McLean, SPCK, 1961. Used by permission of the publishers.

A catalogue record for this book is available
from the British Library

Printed and bound in Great Britain
by Caledonian Manufacturing International, Glasgow

PSALMS 73–150

THE PEOPLE'S BIBLE COMMENTARY

DONALD COGGAN

A BIBLE COMMENTARY FOR EVERY DAY

The Bible Reading Fellowship
OPENING THE BIBLE

EDITORS' FOREWORD

When this series of books was first planned, it was described as a Bible commentary that would speak to 'heart and mind'. Obviously readers need help with understanding and interpreting the text of the Bible, but our hope was that these books would also have as a central aim the *application* of the Bible's message. 'The word of God is living and active... able to judge the thoughts and intentions of the heart,' says the writer to the Hebrews. If the scriptures are in any meaningful sense the 'word of the Lord' then they are more than simply 'books', and they are there not just to be studied and interpreted, but applied to our lives.

When we invited Lord Coggan to contribute to the volumes on the Psalms, we had this aspect of the series very much in mind. As a distinguished Hebrew scholar, and chairman of the joint committee that produced the Revised English Bible, he was eminently qualified to explain and interpret the text of the Psalter. But as one of the great preachers of our time, he would, we felt, also be able to capture the passion and feeling of these remarkable writings and help his readers respond to them with 'heart' as well as 'mind'.

After all the Psalms are not prose, but *poetry*, and poetry requires a quite different approach from historical, narrative or didactic writings. If we miss the 'feel' of a psalm, then we miss its meaning too. In considering these poems, then, questions of authorship and text are interesting, but not as crucial as they may be in other scriptures. Consequently, while they are not ignored, the emphasis in this commentary is on meaning and message.

Two hundred years ago Matthew Henry said of the Psalms that 'none ever comes up so dry from David's well'. This commentary, by one who has known, loved and preached the Psalms all his life, will help us to dip eagerly into that deep and refreshing source.

The Editors

INTRODUCING THE
PEOPLE'S BIBLE COMMENTARY
SERIES

Congratulations! You are embarking on a voyage of discovery—or rediscovery. You may feel you know the Bible very well; you may never have turned its pages before. You may be looking for a fresh way of approaching daily Bible study; you may be searching for useful insights to share in a study group or from a pulpit.

The People's Bible Commentary (PBC) series is designed for all those who want to study the scriptures in a way that will warm the heart as well as instructing the mind. To help you, the series distils the best of scholarly insights into the straightforward language and devotional emphasis of Bible reading notes. Explanation of background material, and discussion of the original Greek and Hebrew, will always aim to be brief.

- If you have never really studied the Bible before, the series offers a serious yet accessible way in.

- If you help to lead a church study group, or are otherwise involved in regular preaching and teaching, you can find invaluable 'snapshots' of a Bible passage through the PBC approach.

- If you are a church worker or minister, burned out on the Bible, this series could help you recover the wonder of scripture.

Using a People's Bible Commentary

The series is designed for use alongside any version of the Bible. You may have your own favourite translation, but you might like to consider trying a different one in order to gain fresh perspectives on familiar passages.

Many Bible translations come in a range of editions, including study and reference editions that have concordances, various kinds of special index, maps and marginal notes. These can all prove helpful in studying the relevant passage. The Notes section at the back of each PBC volume provides space for you to write personal reflections, points to follow up, questions and comments.

Each People's Bible Commentary can be used on a daily basis, instead of Bible reading notes. Alternatively, it can be read straight through, or used as a resource book for insight into particular verses of the biblical book.

If you have enjoyed using this commentary and would like to progress further in Bible study, you will find details of other volumes in the series listed at the back, together with information about a special offer from BRF.

While it is important to deepen understanding of a given passage, this series always aims to engage both heart and mind in the study of the Bible. The scriptures point to our Lord himself and our task is to use them to build our relationship with him. When we read, let us do so prayerfully, slowly, reverently, expecting him to speak to our hearts.

CONTENTS

Acknowledgments

I am grateful to:

David Winter, without whose skill this book might not have seen the light;

Naomi Starkey, who has been his colleague in this work;

Armorel Willmot, who has enabled us to keep to the announced date of publication: amid many calls on her time, attention and skill, she has proved of invaluable help—a help always with a smile;

and Jean, whose encouragement to me in writing this book, and whose love during sixty-four years of married life, have been beyond price.

PBC PSALMS 73–150: INTRODUCTION
Sandals Off!

To open the book of Psalms is to find ourselves confronted by a mystery. The mystery is the fact of their appeal to people of all kinds, and their impact on them irrespective of time or circumstances. Let me illustrate. I begin with the testimony of a young man, a Cambridge graduate, a businessman with very bright prospects in the City of London. He gave it all up to go to Chile to work among the youth of that country and especially among the deprived. At the age of twenty-seven he wrote to his parents:

> My life has been transformed through the discovery of the voice of Christ in Scripture. Indeed, through learning to pray with the Bible a whole new world has opened up before me; where Life and Love are not defined by what suits me or society around me, but by that immeasurable power and presence we call God; and that God calls us to live that love in my own special vocation... I had never before really seen the Bible as a place to meet God... Yet... I found myself consuming the passion and yearning of the psalms that seems to reach across the centuries in my own increasingly desperate desire to know where and who God is. 'As a deer yearns for running streams, so my soul is yearning for you, O God.'

Some sixteen centuries before this, Augustine of Hippo wrote about his experience as a young man when he read the psalms:

> My God, how I cried to you when I read the Psalms of David, songs of faith, utterances of devotion which allow no pride of spirit to enter in! I was but a beginner in authentic love of you... How I cried out to you in those Psalms, and how they kindled my love for you! I was fired by an enthusiasm to recite them, were it possible, to the entire world in protest against the pride of the human race. Yet they are being sung in all the world—'there is none that can hide himself from your heat'. (Confessions)

Dr Allen Wicks, organist and choirmaster of Canterbury Cathedral from 1961 to 1988, has written of 'the tempestuous exhilaration of the psalmists' response to God':

At Canterbury my youthful admiration of the psalms became a passion, fed by the choristers' enthusiasm for these, by turns, trembling, angry, beseeching, challenging, fiery, trusting, accepting, radiant songs directed at Jehovah.

For myself, I have been fairly well acquainted with the psalms since I was a boy. But the writing of this book has brought me into a new relationship with them and, if I may dare say so, with their writers, and, I would hope, with their God and mine. For to understand a psalm, it is necessary to realize that we are treading on holy ground—where the saints have trod down long centuries. Early in his life, Moses came to Horeb, the mountain of God. There he saw the burning bush which was not burnt up. There God spoke to him: 'Do not come near! Take off your sandals, for the place where you are standing is holy ground' (Exodus 3:1–6). To enter into the meaning of the psalms we must take off our sandals. These writers were in touch with the Holy One. Sometimes they raged at him. Sometimes they adored him. Often they consciously did neither, but just got on with living a godly life *with an eye Godwards*. Sometimes they prayed alone, yet not alone, for God was with them. Often they prayed in the company of other faithful souls, in the great services of temple worship or in the less awesome surroundings of the synagogue. But it is 'sandals off!' if the secrets of the psalmists are to be disclosed. We are in touch with the God of Abraham, Isaac and Jacob, with the God and Father of our Lord Jesus Christ (for he used these psalms and made them his own). We are in touch with the spiritual resources of the saints of the ages.

Imagination is needed if the psalms are to release their treasures to us. It is hard to realize how different was the world of the psalmists from our world. Theirs was a world of few books and no phones, e-mail or TV screens; a pastoral world, not one of tower-blocks and concrete; a world of flocks and cattle, not of investments; a world of country paths, not of macadamized streets; a tiny world far removed from any concept of travel in space, of light-years or of evolutionary processes. It might be thought that anything they wrote, or any poems which they handed down from generation to generation, would be so far removed from us as to be almost wholly worthless. But this is not so, and the reason is not far to seek. These ancient writers share with us a common humanity, and their writings touch

14

our hearts and minds precisely because they deal with matters which most deeply affect us as human beings. Justice in a world where injustice reigns; relationships with God, with one another, with foreigners, with wicked people; love and hate; sickness and depression; sin and forgiveness—these are the stuff of which our humanity is made. These are the problems that torture us and tease us, whether we live in the year 2000BC or AD2000. Basically, we and the psalmists are one.

With sandals off, then, and imagination at the ready, you begin to read a psalm. Don't look for logic. The writer is not a scientist, at pains to watch every syllable he writes lest he get a fact wrong. Here are people in agony. Here are people exuberant. Here are people at moments of high spiritual experience. Don't look for logic. Rather, listen for a heartbeat. And remember that you are in the world of poetry—these psalms are *poems*, and poems need *time*...

This raises a matter of importance in the use of this book. Please do not try to 'do' one psalm a day. In the *New Daylight* Bible reading notes of the Bible Reading Fellowship, there is a brief passage of scripture and a comment for one day—and we move on to the next. This is not the purpose of these two volumes on the psalms. I hope you will work your way through them, but not that you will finish in 150 days! You will notice that some comments are longer than others. I had to linger on one psalm before I went on to the next. I hope you will do the same. If a psalm is meeting your need or challenging your assumptions, stay with it, take your time with it. Chew the cud. 'Let yourself be filled' by a psalm or by a verse or a phrase in it. Meditate on it. Let it keep you company through a day, or even in the hours of a sleepless night, or on a walk. To use a phrase of the Chief Rabbi Jonathan Sacks: 'Create a space for the Shekinah' (God's presence).

The one and the many

There is an extraordinary intimacy which marks many of the psalms—the intimacy of a person's relationship with the Holy One. We notice it, for example, in Psalm 18:1, when we see in our mind's eye a frail mortal looking up into the face of the Almighty and saying: 'I love you, Lord.' Or again in Psalm 42:1–2, when the psalmist says: 'As a hind longs for the running streams, so I long for you, my God. I thirst for God...' Or again, there is intimacy, the intimacy of a *break* of relationship and a sense of dereliction, when the psalmist cries out:

'My God, my God, why have you forsaken me?' (Psalm 22:1). By way of contrast, we look at the opening verses of Psalm 103, and find the psalmist calling on himself to 'bless the Lord' who has so blessed him in pardoning him, healing him, rescuing him, satisfying him. In Psalm 34:8 he bids the people share the satisfaction which he himself has found in God—'Taste and see that the Lord is good'.

The writers are in touch with the living God. Each writer can only tell the world how it is with *him*. How can a couple, head over heels in love, convey their experience to their friends? When they attempt to do so, they can only stutter, or write a poem, or sing a song…

We cannot begin to express our relationship with God without the use of personal pronouns—he… me… What a revelation it was when Saul of Tarsus came to realize that 'the Son of God… loved *me* and gave himself up for *me*' (Galatians 2:20)! When Augustine pondered on the power of his mother's prayers in leading him out of the clutches of his old life into one made new in Christ, he said to God: 'You are good and all-powerful, *caring for each one of us as though the only one in your care*' (*Confessions* III.xi.19).

God, who is love, takes the initiative. A human being responds, sometimes very haltingly, but contact is made. That is where intimacy can be found, and the psalms are full of it.

But there is another element in the psalms, equally strong, equally pervasive. It is the sense of community. Religion for those writers is not 'the flight of the alone to the Alone'. Far from it. They write from the perspective of people who are what they are precisely because they are members of a nation which believes itself to have a special relationship with God. He has created this nation, revealed himself to it, called it, stayed with it in all its sufferings, sent it on his mission to the world. The psalmists write as members of the people of God.

The people had received a Law, a teaching, which they were not only committed to obey and live by, but of which they were also trustees. The figure of Moses towers over the writings of the Old Testament. Obedience to the law that was given on Sinai led to prosperity (in the fullness of that word's meaning). Disobedience led to death and disaster. To receive that teaching and to pass it on faithfully was not the road to bondage or sterility. Rather, the reverse. Hence the note of joy and privilege which characterizes such a psalm as 119: 'In your commandments I find continuing delight; I love them with all my heart' (v. 47).

The psalms are the writings of members of a nation that was unique—unique in its sense of trusteeship, not in the sense of perfection. The story of Israel, the people of God, is one marred by constant failure, disobedience, contamination from polytheistic neighbours. But always there was a remnant which was loyal and through whom God would work out his purposes. The community might be small. Its purpose never changed.

The outstanding mark of this people of God was that it was a *worshipping* community. During the long, weary years of wandering in the wilderness, the focus of their worship was the Tent of Meeting, marked by the pillar of cloud by day and of fire by night (see notes on Psalm 15). There God met with his people (see Exodus 25). There they learned the lessons of awe-full worship. When at last they settled in the land which God had promised them, tent worship gave way to temple worship. The first temple having been destroyed around 586BC, the building of the second temple was undertaken some six decades later. The prophecies of Haggai and Zechariah in which these men urged the work forward make interesting reading. In 167BC Antiochus Epiphanes desecrated the temple by offering a pig on its altar. Judas Maccabaeus, with enormous courage, supervised its re-dedication in 164BC, and the reconstruction of this magnificent building, supported by Herod the Great, was still in process when Jesus taught in its courts during his ministry.

Here the sacrifice of vast numbers of sheep and cattle went on in ceaseless succession. Here the tribes of the Lord went up to worship at the great feasts. Here music of all kinds accompanied the songs of the worshippers (see, for example, Psalm 150:3–6). The book of Psalms, much as we now have it, has justifiably been called 'the hymn-book of the second temple'. Its title in Hebrew is simply 'Praises'. No wonder that Jerusalem, the city where all this took place, has, from that day to this, evoked the deepest and most passionate feelings of love and loyalty. This was 'the city of God, the holy dwelling of the Most High; God is in her midst...' (Psalm 46:4, 5). 'His holy mountain is fair and lofty, the joy of the whole earth. The mountain of Zion... is the city of the great King' (Psalm 48:1, 2). 'Lord of Hosts,' cried one worshipper, 'how dearly loved is your dwelling place! I pine and faint with longing for the courts of the Lord's temple; my whole being cries out with joy to the living God' (Psalm 84:1, 2). 'I rejoiced,' said another worshipper, 'when they said to me, "Let us go to the house of the Lord." Now we are standing within your gates, Jerusalem: Jerusalem, a city built compactly and solidly' (Psalm 122:1–3).

The sheer solidity of the building, with its massive stones, spoke of the solidity of the promises of the God who entered into a covenant relationship with his people; the beauty of its construction and adornment, its golden doors shimmering in the light of the rising sun, spoke of his majesty and grace. One greater than any of the prophets, as he entered the city which had rejected him, God's supreme ambassador, broke down and wept: 'O Jerusalem, Jerusalem... How often have I longed to gather your children... but you would not let me' (Luke 13:34).

Worship, joyful worship, musical worship, corporate worship was at the centre of the life of the people of God; worship which led to upright and godly living. 'Lord, who may lodge in your tent? Who may dwell on your holy mountain? One of blameless life... (Psalm 15:1, 2). In reading the psalms we learn much about the warmth and dynamism of Jewish worship and, if we have ears to hear, about Israel's God, creator, redeemer, King.

Text and authorship

If you compare the text of the Revised English Bible, which we are using, with that of the Authorized Version (1611) or the Prayer Book Version, you will notice very considerable differences in the translation. A good example would be Psalm 87. Why is this? Because in the passing down of this psalm, as indeed in many of them, the work of copying by hand has necessarily involved errors. Scholars have faced these difficulties, and given the best translations that they can, often making sense of a verse which in earlier versions made little or no sense at all.

It must be borne in mind that this book is not a verse-by-verse commentary. A series of volumes would be needed for that purpose—and there are many already on the scholars' shelves. Here we have often been bound to leave puzzling words or phrases without comment—that is regrettable but unavoidable. I have tried to convey the general 'feel' of the psalm and of the person who wrote it—to look at the poem through the eyes of the poet, and to get to the heart of its permanent message. If this leaves the reader to search in the commentaries for light on the details, so much the better.

'The person who wrote it... the eyes of the poet'. Who did write these psalms? Whose were the eyes of the poets? These are questions which admit of no easy answers. 'The Psalms of David' will not do, for clearly in the Psalter (the psalms as we now have them) we have a collection of poems by a wide variety of people. The headings of the psalms are not part of the original poems—they were added later. Some of them are headed 'for David', or it might be 'by David'. Some headings link the poem with some particular incident in David's career. Psalm 51 is a case in point, linking as it does David's adultery with Bathsheba (see 2 Samuel 11 and 12) with his broken-hearted penitence. That link adds special point both to the incident and to the psalm. 'The sweet psalmist of Israel' (2 Samuel 23:1, Authorized Version), 'the singer of Israel's psalms' (Revised English Bible) may well have been the author of the psalms as well as the singer or accompanist of them.

What is clear is that we have in the collection a hymn-book of the people of God. As we read or chant these psalms we see a people at worship, communities of faith in the one and only God, at grips with him while being (many of them) surrounded by worshippers of wood and stone, holding on to their faith against all the odds of polytheistic counter-attractions. A collection, in the nature of the case, takes many years to come together; we have in these one hundred and fifty poems works from many centuries of Israel's experience—hence the rich mixture of despair and hope, of complaint and praise. The whole gamut of a nation's experience is reflected here, as well as a wide range of the joys and agonies of individuals.

Many of the psalms are intended to be set to music—hence the rich variety of instruments mentioned in them (see, for example, 150:3–5). The oft-recurring *Hallelujah* is probably a direction to the congregation to take its vocal part. And the word *lamenasseah* in the headings of some psalms, although its meaning is obscure, was very likely a musical direction. So the word *selah*, which is printed in the body of the text of many psalms, was probably a direction to the choir or musicians to 'strike up' (for example, in 3:2, 4).

The Psalter is divided into five books: 1—41; 42—72; 73—89; 90—106; 107—150. In this volume we consider the last three books (73—150), the first two being covered in a previous volume.

There are two instances of duplication within the Psalter. Psalm 14 and Psalm 53 are virtually identical. Likewise, Psalm 40:13–17 is repeated almost word for word in Psalm 70. Such duplication may suggest that the five books of psalms may have been used separately, by different communities, and were later brought together to form the Psalter as we know it.

There is a wide variety of types in the Psalter as it has come down to us. There are psalms of complaint or lament, which are wrung from the heart of the writer as he thinks of his distress, sin or sickness (for example, 22; 38; 42—43). There are psalms of praise and exhilaration, songs of Zion, confident in the presence of the Lord in Jerusalem (for example, 46; 84; 122). There are royal psalms which celebrate the king as God's regent (for example, 2; 20; 45; 72). There are enthronement psalms in which the kingship of God is dwelt on (for example, 47; 93; 95—99). There are wisdom psalms which remind us of the book of Proverbs and (in the Apocrypha) the book of Wisdom (for example, 34; 37). Some psalms are obviously for individual use, some for corporate worship. This should be borne in mind as each psalm is studied.

The authors of the psalms delighted in the use of parallelism, that is to say, the second part of the verse virtually repeats the first in order to underline it, deepen it or elaborate it. Or the second part of the verse may serve to make a contrast with the first, as in 1:6:

The Lord watches over the way of the righteous,
  but the way of the wicked is doomed.

Some of the psalms are *acrostic*, with each verse or section beginning with a different letter of the Hebrew alphabet, the most elaborate being 119, with eight verses for each of the twenty-two letters of the Hebrew alphabet—quite a feat!

All these things (and a dozen others on which we have no space to comment) add interest to the poems we are about to study. But they are trivial compared to this point which we must always bear in mind: the value of the psalms lies in the fact that they face us constantly with the great major concepts which are Israel's distinctive gift to the world and for which we Christians are in everlasting debt to Israel—the righteousness of God; the loving compassion of God; the covenant-relationship between God and his people; the Law (teaching) of God; the yearning of the human heart for God; his yearning for us.

Imprecatory psalms

A special note is called for on the so-called imprecatory or cursing psalms.

At various points in this book we shall come across psalms, or parts of psalms, which are called 'imprecatory' or 'cursing' (for example, 58; 68:21–23; 69:22–28; 109:8–20; 137:7–9). I have thought it best to mention them here, rather than repeatedly comment on them as they occur.

In many prayer books they are bracketed as being unsuitable for use in public worship. There is much to be said for this. In the course of public worship they cannot be commented on, and their recitation only occasions offence or even revulsion on the part of those who are genuinely seeking to worship God.

But they are part and parcel of these poems, and it will not do simply to put our (mental) pen through the offending psalms and, by omitting them, to say in effect: 'We know better than the psalmists did. Did not Jesus say, "Love your enemies and pray for your persecutors" (Matthew 5:44), and did not Paul say, "My dear friends, do not seek revenge..." (Romans 12:19)? These passages are regrettable. Forget them!' We must go deeper than this.

It is not correct to describe these psalms as cursing psalms. The psalmists do not curse their enemies—they call on God to deal with the persons who have offended. They lament in passionate terms. They petition God. To transfer the vengeance which they feel on to God is to renounce their own vengeance, and that could be a cathartic experience for them.

Two positive points must be made. The first about the situation in which the psalmists found themselves and which gave rise to such violent reaction; the second about the character of the God to whom they address their prayers.

Firstly, we need to remember that the background of these psalms is not one of monastic or domestic calm, but one of extreme violence. The writers have reached a point of endurance beyond which they cannot go. No conventional means of justice is adequate for the situation in which they find themselves. Theirs is a violent age, and they or their loved ones are the victims of that violence. This is not difficult for us to appreciate today. We live in an age of violence. We see that violence wreaked on innocent children—raped, abused, hit by drunken drivers... We read the comments of their parents: 'May they burn in hell for ever.' Conventional churchgoers are shocked by such reactions. But is there not in all of us some measure of fellow-feeling?

The psalmists are passionate people. They feel, and they put their feelings into words. But they know where to turn *in extremis*. They turn to God. They are driven to the Holy One. Let him deal with the situation—vengeance is *his* concern! They pray, and their prayer may not be much better than an angry blurt. But at the end, they can sing—or most of them can!

Secondly, we must reflect on what sort of God it is that they pray to. What is his character? He is a God who is concerned about real-life situations. His name is Yahweh ('I am what I am' or 'I will be what I will be'). He will make himself known by what he does. He is the Just One who is concerned for human justice. He is grieved about his creation when it goes wrong, about his creatures when his image in them is defaced and they 'fall short of the glory of God' (Romans 3:23, NRSV). A place must be left for divine retribution (Romans 12:19).

Imagine yourself in a situation like that of the psalmists. You have been deeply injured, offended, hurt. What courses of action are open to you? On the one hand, you can internalize your feelings—'let them burn in hell'. But if you do that, the odds are that you will damage yourself more than you will damage them. You will remain bitter, and you will be nervously and quite possibly physically damaged. On the other hand, you can externalize your feelings. You can tell God not only what you feel but also what you would do if you were in control of the situation. Get it off your chest. Tell him— if that is how you feel—that you would congratulate the person who seized their babes and dashed them against a rock (Psalm 137:9). Ask God to act—and leave the timing to him. Your language, when you come back later to look at it, may have been revolting, shocking. But God's back is strong enough to bear it and to deal with it. The God in whose hands you have decided to leave things is the Judge. But he is also the Saviour. His judgment, fearful though it is, is creative. His reaction to sin is not to be thought of in terms of offended dignity, but rather of outraged love.

I am conscious that this introduction leaves many questions unanswered. But at least it offers an approach which takes the problem seriously and deserves following up.

In this book, I do not refer readers to many books on the psalms.

I want them to study the psalms themselves, the text being open before them. Commentaries can wait. But in the context of the imprecatory psalms I mention two books which I have found helpful: Walter Brueggeman's *Praying the Psalms* (St Mary's Press, Christian Book Publications) and Eric Zenger's *A God of Vengeance. Understanding the Psalms of Divine Wrath* (Westminster/John Knox Press).

Psalms 73—150

Book III of the Psalms (73—89) opens with a group which all have 'for Asaph' at their head (73—82). We shall note other groups of psalms, for example 120—135, which are called 'Songs of Ascent'; and 113—118 and 146—150 which are 'alleluia' psalms. 'Songs of Ascent' were probably sung as worshippers made their way in procession up the long steps to the temple. 'Alleluia' psalms were simply songs of praise—'alleluia' means 'praise the Lord'.

There is an interesting passage in 1 Chronicles 25:1ff. in which 'the sons of Asaph' with other musicians were assigned special musical duties in the Temple, 'master-singer and apprentices side by side'. Presumably these were guilds of singers and instrumentalists who led the people in their worship of God.

The PROBLEM *of* EVIL

There is a surprising intimacy about Psalm 73. The writer invites us to share with him his experience of God, an experience at once of perplexity and of near relationship.

The psalm opens on a note of joy—God is good! It ends with a passage which describes God's dealings with the psalmist and his dealings with God (vv. 23–28), a passage so deep and intimate as to have few parallels in the Old Testament—'I am always with you... you guide me... my chief good is to be near you... I have chosen you, Lord God...'

But there is a long passage between the opening and closing verses which strikes a sombre note. The writer faces the problem of evil—a reality so stark as to shake his faith and to lead him to question the validity of his religious experience. Why do the wicked prosper? They get away with murder—'unshakeably secure' (v. 12), and are oblivious to God's knowledge of their evil lives (v. 11). The psalmist, on the other hand, suffers affliction, and every morning brings him new punishment (v. 14). It is a situation which brings him near to despair, *until* (v. 17) ... until he does the sensible thing and withdraws from his self-pity into the place where he can pray and think—'God's sanctuary'. *There* he gets his perspectives right. There he sees that evil has at its heart the seeds of decay; the bully-boys are bent on destruction, but their triumphs will be blotted out. There is no future for ungodliness. With his limited ideas of an after-life, the psalmist finds a partial answer, but there are many questions left unanswered—his 'mind is embittered', his heart pierced (v. 21). We have great sympathy with him. There is a mystery about iniquity which remains unsolved even with the light that comes from resurrection triumph and final hope. There are no easy answers even for us. 'You do not understand now what I am doing, but one day you will,' as Jesus said to his disciples at the last supper when they were confused and anxious (John 13:7).

God is near

Against that dark and perplexing background, the psalmist comes to the reality of religious experience. His 'feet had almost slipped' (v. 2), but God was near, holding his right hand (v. 23), guiding him with his counsel (v. 24); God is the rock of his heart (v. 26). 'Afterwards you will receive me with glory' (v. 24). We do not know what that meant to the psalmist, but we do know what it means to the Christian. It means that God, having begun a good work in us, will not give it up until that work is completed. It means that one day we shall see face to face. The apostle Paul looked forward to that moment: 'My knowledge now is partial; then it will be whole' (1 Corinthians 13:12). For John, this would be the moment of completion, of perfection: 'We shall be like him, because we shall see him as he is' (1 John 3:2).

Meanwhile, 'my chief good is to be near you, God' (v. 28). The Scottish Catechism got it right when it said, 'The chief end of man is to glorify God and enjoy him for ever.'

In Francis Jackson's biography of Edward C. Bairstow, we hear how the great organist of York Minster was often on the verge of tears as he accompanied the psalms:

Perhaps this was why he accompanied them as nobody else did, or could, or perhaps ever will. These two verses [vv. 23, 24] remained his inspiration. They reveal the secret of his life and of his influence over his fellow men, through the divine gift of music. 'Nevertheless I am always by thee: for thou hast holden me by my right hand. Thou shalt guide me with thy counsel: and after that receive me with glory.'

(Blessed City: The Life and Works of Edward C. Bairstow, p. 231).

PRAISE

My knowledge of that life is small,
The eye of faith is dim;
But 'tis enough that Christ knows all,
And I shall be with him.

R. Baxter (1615–91)

The TEMPLE DESTROYED

The writer of this psalm gives a terribly vivid description of the temple after its destruction. (There is a similar description of the temple defiled and the city of Jerusalem in ruins in Psalm 79:1–4.) We can almost hear the shouts of the enemy as they profaned the sanctuary of the Most High God: the ripping out of the carvings; the pollution of the abode of the Holy One; the crackle of the destroying fires. We do not know with any certainty the date of this psalm, whether it is telling us of the destruction of Solomon's temple by the Babylonians in 587BC, or the desecration of the holy place by Antiochus in 168BC. For our purposes it matters little. The awful fact stares us in the face in verses 4–8.

The physical facts lead to theological questionings—where is God in all this (v. 1)? It would seem that God has cast off his people—is this for ever? Is there to be no redress or relief? We note the bitter repetition of these questions in verse 10. It all sounds so modern— where was God at Auschwitz? The situation is made the more dire in that there seems to be no word from God—'we have no prophet now'. Famine often comes in the wake of invasion; that is a fact of history. But here is famine of another and more awful kind—a famine of a word from God. Amos envisages such a situation—people ranging 'from north to east, in search of the word of the Lord', but unable to find it. That is the ultimate famine horror (Amos 8:11–12).

A sea of doubt and despair

Can God's people survive without a temple, without prophets? The psalmist throws himself back on God (vv. 12ff.), the God who in the act of creation conquered the 'monster' of original chaos, the 'deep' of Genesis 1:2. The mythological language of the conquest of the sea-serpent, Leviathan, appears again in Isaiah 51:9–10, and is used to convey the power of the 'arm of the Lord'. Israel's God is the God of creation who 'ordered the light of moon and sun', who 'created both summer and winter'—the language reminds us of the creation stories of Genesis—the God who created order out of primeval chaos and who can be trusted to do so again. As we have seen in other psalms, part of this 'trust' in Jewish thought is concerned with God's vindication of the innocent victims of injustice, and his punishment of their oppressors, the 'wicked'. The last half of this psalm has within it shafts of the light of faith and hope, but the psalmist expresses himself through both halves as the man of faith who wrestles his way through a sea of doubt and despair.

TO PONDER

Jim Cotter, in a moving poem on this psalm, heads it 'The Sea of Faith?' The first stanza runs:

The more we are aware, O God,
the harder does faith become.
The more we contemplate the desolation,
the further we seem to withdraw.

He ends with these three stanzas:

Work on this earth of your creating,
see the billowing clouds of corruption,
Listen to the trudge of the weary,
open your ears to the accents of the mindless.

Dare we praise you, O God, do you hear our cry,
meeting it in the depths of your being,
giving yourself for us and all people,
the Lamb slain across aeons of time?

To the mystery of the Cross we hurl our questions,
and doggedly worry away at our doubts.
Yes, you absorb the wastes of our wraths and sorrows,
turning from pain to glory in the vortex of Love.

From *By Stony Paths*, Cairns Publications, 1991

The LORD IS NEAR

Verse 1: 'your name' (your character, what you essentially are) 'is brought very near to us'. There is a delightful passage in Deuteronomy 30:11–14, in which Moses, about to die, is depicted as summing up the way of life which God has made clear to his people in the commandment which he has given. 'It is not too difficult for you or beyond your reach,' he says. 'It is not in the heavens, that you should say, "Who will go up to the heavens for us to fetch it... so that we can keep it?" Nor is it beyond the sea, that you should say, "Who will cross the sea for us to fetch it... so that we can keep it?" It is a thing very near to you... ready to be kept.' As our psalmist says, 'Your name is brought very near to us...' To put this in Christian terms, we can say, 'In the person and work of Jesus, crucified and risen, God has made known his name, what he essentially is. He has come very near to us.' Life lived in obedience to his declared mind and will is life as God intends it to be. It is not found in theorizing about him; it is found in obedience to him, in response to 'your wonderful deeds'. Those 'deeds' to the Israelites meant especially the rescue of God's people from the tyranny of Egyptian domination. Those 'deeds' to the Christian mean God's rescue of his people from the tyranny of sin and death through the mighty acts of Christ himself.

God's words

The speaker of verses 2–5 is, of course, God himself. The rest of the psalm consists of the comments of the psalmist on those words of authority (vv. 2–3) and of rebuke and warning (vv. 4–5). (Verse 3 reminds us of Psalm 46:1–3: see comment on these verses). It is human pride which blinds our eyes to the majesty and ultimate authority of God, 'Disposer Supreme and Judge of the earth'. That is, of course, the theme of verses 6 and 7: 'For God is ruler; he puts one down, another he raises up.'

Verse 8: what a picture of God! He has in his hand a cup of wine, foaming and full of flavour. He pours it out and offers it. What more joyful and exhilarating gift could there be? But this, intended for our delight, becomes for the ungodly, greedy and intoxicated, a deadly drink, and they find the God of grace and mercy to be a God of judgment. The psalmist draws his illustration from the world of taste; Paul has a somewhat similar illustration from the world of scent, in a passage where he writes of the Christ-event as 'a vital fragrance that brings life' to those 'on the way to salvation', but 'a deadly fume' to 'those who are on the way to destruction' (2 Corinthians 2:15–16). To the proud and self-sufficient, God's wisdom, revealed in his Son, is sheer folly. To the believer, it is life itself with joy unspeakable and full of glory.

The tragedy of human history lies in our ability to misuse God's loveliest gifts—so that wine leads to debauchery, harmony to discord, sexual joy to selfish indulgence.

PRAYER

As we pray for a world full of man-made gods and maddened by the cacophony of Godlessness, our only prayer can be:

Lord, have mercy. Christ, have mercy. Lord, have mercy.

or

Holy God,
Holy and strong,
Holy and immortal,
have mercy on us.

PSALM 76

POWER & BEAUTY

Awe is a difficult word to define. It is best understood by way of illustration. I have had the privilege, repeated several times, of visiting the Canadian Rockies. The majesty of those snow-covered peaks is indescribable. Only once have I visited the Grand Canyon in the United States of America. There I have stood in silent wonder before that great ravine, carved out, over the course of millions of years, by the forces of flowing water. Such experiences, we say, are awe-inspiring. The most garrulous of us are left speechless, reduced (or is it raised?) to silence by the sight of power and beauty. We are in the presence of the *awesome*.

To define awe as 'overwhelming wonder, respect or dread' is to include a personal element. To stand in awe of somebody is to wonder at her, respect her (or, perhaps, to dread her). Awe is next to wonder, and wonder is next to worship. Something like this moved our psalmist to write as he did: 'You are awesome, Lord' (v. 4). He repeats the sentence (v. 7). He refers to it a third time in verse 12—even kings are filled with awe before the majesty of Israel's God.

It was not so much the majesty of God as revealed in nature that moved our psalmist (though there is a nature reference in verse 4). It was some event in recent history (not defined)—'In Judah God is known, his name is great in Israel' (v. 1)—when God had manifested his power in defeating Israel's enemies, by breaking the flashing arrows of the enemy, their shields and swords and weapons of war (v. 3). The language reminds us of Psalm 46:9. God had given 'sentence out of heaven' (v. 8), risen in judgment and delivered the afflicted (v. 9). The petty surrounding nations—Edom to the south-east and Hamath to the north—were led to praise and to worship God as a result (v. 10).

Too much talk

The concept of awe is a particularly difficult one for people living at the end of the twentieth century to get their teeth into. The great institutions of our society—the Church, the Law included—are lampooned in the media. That may be good for the institutions concerned, for it may alert them to their faults or weaknesses. It is more dangerous for those who do the lampooning, for the Church and the Law stand for certain values without which society will collapse. We talk too much. We think, we respect, we wonder too little.

To turn to another aspect of life: in public worship we talk too much and wonder too little. Does the Eucharist or the Service of the Word reduce me (or should we say raise me?) to silence, to wonder, to respect? 'You are awesome, Lord.' If that is recognized, there will be silence before the entry of the ministers. There will be times of silence during the service—'I will hearken to what God the Lord will say.'

PRAYER

Let all mortal flesh keep silence
And with fear and trembling stand;
Ponder nothing earthly-minded,
For with blessing in his hand
Christ our God to earth descendeth,
Our full homage to demand.

G. Moultrie (1829–85)

A FRAGMENT *of* AUTOBIOGRAPHY

It seems pretty clear that we have in this psalm the description of a specific period in the writer's life, a fragment of autobiography. He invites us to share his experience in a time of deep depression—'the day of my distress', 'my tears' (v. 2), 'I groaned' (v. 3), 'I was distraught' (v. 4), 'I remembered… I meditated… I pondered' (vv. 5, 6). His depression (v. 2) leads him to question the validity of his religious experience: has God rejected him (v. 7)? Has God's love run out (v. 8)? Is God angry with him (v. 9)? Or—this is surely the worst possibility—is God simply powerless (v. 10)?

There is no suggestion of his sharing his depression with others. Mercifully, he has no comforters such as Job had. Mercifully, there is no one to say 'Snap out of it'—surely the most fatuous advice to give to someone in the throes of grief! Nor does he find an easy solution of his problems. But there are indications that all is not totally black for him as time goes by. There are shafts of light in the darkness. They begin to appear at verse 11 and go on to the end of the psalm.

Shafts of light

What causes these shafts of light? He cannot get away from the facts of history. Perhaps the God who made a way out for Israel from the hand of her oppressors might find a way out for him? The psalmist does not tell us what actually happened to him, but there is enough in these verses (11–20) to give us good hope that he came through into the sunshine.

Relief came to him as he 'called to mind the deeds of the Lord' (v. 11), particularly in the events of the Exodus (vv. 16–19). With poetic licence, he describes how God loosed from Pharaoh's bitter yoke

Jacob's sons and daughters;
led them with unmoistened foot
through the Red Sea waters.

The psalmist cannot get away from the holiness of God, the greatness of God, the power of God (vv. 11–15) and, surely, the tenderness of the God who, when the Red Sea had been crossed, guided his people through their long wilderness wanderings, using Moses and Aaron as his shepherds (v. 20). Through the dark clouds of depression, he caught a glimpse of the changelessness of God, and therein he began to find rest and hope—words of reassurance not only to the psalmist but, surely, to the present-day reader as well.

PRAYER

Guide me, O thou great Redeemer,
Pilgrim through this barren land;
I am weak, but thou art mighty;
Hold me with thy powerful hand:
Bread of heaven,
Feed me now and evermore.

P. Williams (1721–96) and W. Williams (1717–91)

Lessons *from a* Great Teacher

In this long psalm we can see a great teacher at work. He is clearly in a position of some authority—he addresses his audience as 'my people' (v. 1). He is concerned that Israel's history should be preserved: tradition, the handing down of a nation's story, its customs and its life, can easily become corrupt. It matters. But this psalm is far more than a history lesson. It is a meditation on the significance of the story—a saga of events told in such a way that succeeding generations will see its meaning and pass it on to their successors (vv. 4–6). God has made known his nature and will; those who listen to the teaching are trustees of the truth for the generations to come.

There can be no doubt about the central figure in this saga. It is God himself. God is presented as a God of judgment and of faithfulness to his declared will. Israel is presented as a people often faithless, fickle in their allegiance to God, and regardless of the destiny which their Creator has in mind.

The language used to describe God—his patience tried (v. 18), his anger blazing (vv. 21, 31), spreading death (vv. 31, 34), sending plagues (vv. 43ff.), unleashing blazing anger, wrath, enmity and rage (v. 49), offensive as it must seem to those whose picture of God is seen through the life and teaching of Jesus—is to a degree softened within this psalm by reference to God's mercy (v. 38), his consideration for our frailty (v. 39), and his pastoral care (vv. 52ff.). If you want a case of anthropomorphism (speaking of God in human language), verse 65 will be hard to beat—the comparison of the Lord to a sleeper who wakes or a warrior who has had too much to drink. A poet must be allowed his measure of licence!

A suggestion

If readers of this book find that their knowledge of the Old Testament has grown rusty, or realize that the Old Testament is more or less uncharted territory as far as they are concerned, they could undergo a little refresher course by reading the passages which our psalmist clearly had in mind as he wrote of God's dealings with his people. For example, verses 5–8 would send them to Exodus 19—24; verses 12ff. to Exodus 14; verses 15–22 to Numbers 20; verses 23ff. to

Exodus 16 and Numbers 11, and so on. Israel's teachers were great story-tellers, dramatic in their presentation of events. Psalm 78 constitutes a warning never to forget 'the praiseworthy acts of the Lord and the wonders he has done' (v. 4).

A model

The psalm reaches its climax with the appearance of the great figure of David (vv. 67–72). The writer no doubt had in mind the choice of the shepherd-boy as recorded in 1 Samuel 16:1–13. He was the great king from whose line the Christ would come. But here no battles or conquests or achievements are mentioned—simply the shepherding of God's people. When in 1956 I preached in Bradford Cathedral at my own installation, I took as my text the last verse of this psalm and preached on the Prayer Book version of it: 'He fed them with a faithful and true heart and ruled them prudently with all his power.' How better could the office and work of a bishop in the Church of God be described than in this verse—or, for that matter, the calling of any leader in the Church? Here are the qualities of faithful and caring pastoral work and the exercise of discipline combined with prudence. We owe a debt of gratitude to our teacher-historian-theologian-poet man of God for giving us this model of leadership.

TO PONDER

We criticize our spiritual leaders. We have the right to do so. But our motto should be 'one in ten'—for every criticism ten prayers. The old Ember Day hymn suggests how we might direct our prayers:

Wisdom and zeal and faith impart,
Firmness with meekness, from above,
To bear thy people in their heart,
And love the souls whom thou dost love;

To watch and pray and never faint,
By day and night their guard to keep,
To warn the sinner, cheer the saint,
To feed thy lambs and tend thy sheep.

James Montgomery (1771–1854)

BITTERNESS & PASSION

The best way to appreciate the bitterness and the passion of this psalm is to read 2 Kings 24:10—25:21. It is the story of the destruction of Jerusalem and its temple in 587BC—the flight of King Zedekiah of Jerusalem, the slaughter of his sons, the cruelty of the Babylonians in putting out Zedekiah's eyes, the burning of the temple, the theft of its contents, the razing of the city walls. When we have read those chapters and, in addition, Psalm 137, we shall appreciate the horror which led the author of Psalm 79 to write as he did: see especially verses 1–4. (It would seem that this psalm was used on the anniversaries of the events of 587BC—it is quoted in part in 1 Maccabees 7:17, in our Apocrypha.)

Our psalmist sees the national disaster as God's punishment for the nation's sins. But, he would seem to say in protest to God, how long is this punishment going to last? If God's wrath has to be vented on somebody, why not vent it on the Babylonians? (vv. 6 and 12). It's about time we had a bit of mercy from on high (v. 8).

There is an angry hint from the writer that if there is no let-up in the disaster with which God is afflicting his people, he had better look out for his own reputation! The honour of his name (v. 9, twice) is at stake. After all, it is 'your domain', 'your holy temple' that has been invaded and defiled (v. 1). On you the neighbouring enemies pour their contempt (v. 12).

Where is God?

The writer would have understood and appreciated the cry wrung from the lips of the Jews on their way to the extermination camps: 'Where was God at Auschwitz?' Genocide was a word which had to wait for its birth until the twentieth century. But the deportation and the horrors connected with the destruction of Jerusalem in 587BC were bad enough to lead to the bitterness of this psalm, and to the cry 'How long... how long?' (v. 5).

'The groaning of the captives' (v. 11) has a horribly modern ring to it. It is true that, in the history of the human race, there have never been at one time so many prisoners unjustly serving prison sentences and physical and mental torture as there are now. We have only to read the literature of such societies as Prisoners Abroad and Christian Solidarity Worldwide to get a glimpse of the present world picture. The enormity of man's inhumanity to man is hard to conceive.

A tender note

The psalm ends on a more tender note. It is a relief to turn from disaster and bloodshed to the metaphor, beloved by so many Biblical writers, of the shepherd and his flock, and to the mention of thanks and praise (v. 13). God's people are in the hands of a faithful and strong shepherd—'the Shepherd and Guardian of your souls' (1 Peter 2:25). The theme is picked up and elaborated in the next psalm.

PRAYER

Have mercy on your people,
for whom your Son laid down his life...
Look in mercy on all who suffer,
and hear those who cry out in pain and desolation...
Bring comfort to the dying,
and gladden their hearts with the power of your glory.

From *Celebrating Common Prayer*

PSALM 80

The PRAYER of a PATRIOT

This is the prayer of a patriot (see also Psalm 85), deeply concerned at the plight of his people. We note the refrain—'God, restore us, and make your face shine on us, that we may be saved' (vv. 3, 7, 19). The God to whom he prays is thought of as Shepherd and as Vinedresser.

Shepherd

This is a favourite way of conceiving God's relationship with his people—in personal terms ('The Lord is my shepherd', 23:1) and in national terms. Nor is this a matter for surprise—shepherding was one of the main 'industries' of Israel in biblical times. Sheep must be reared for human consumption and for the temple sacrifices. In those days, the work entailed protecting the flock from marauding beasts— David tells Saul, 'I am my father's shepherd; whenever a lion or bear comes and carries off a sheep from the flock, I go out after it and attack it and rescue the victim from its jaws' (1 Samuel 17:34–35).

The shepherd *leads* the flock (vv. 1, 2). Unlike his British counterpart, he goes *before* the sheep, threading a path for them through mountain, gorge or valley. In John's picture of the Good Shepherd, he 'leads them out... he goes ahead of them and the sheep follow' (John 10:3, 4).

The psalmist adds a touch of majesty to his picture of the Shepherd-God. He 'sits enthroned on the cherubim'. We are thus taken into the presence of the Holy One. On the cherubim overshadowing the Ark, see Exodus 25:22: 'It is there that I shall meet you', and see commentary on Psalm 132.

Vinedresser

This again is a favourite way of conceiving God—Israel is the vine; God is the one who plants it, tends it, prunes it. Isaiah 5:1–7 expounds the picture in detail, underlining God's sadness and disappointment at Israel's lack of response to his care. On Jesus as the true vine, the disciples as the branches, and the Father as the gardener, see John 15:1ff.

The story of the Exodus, of God's rescue of his people from Egypt's domination, of the luxuriant growth of the nation (vv. 8–11), contrasts with the pathetic state of the nation when the psalmist wrote. He seems to blame God for the tragedy (v. 12), and he pleads with God to tend that which his right hand has planted (vv. 14, 15). He weeps at the disrepair of God's vine.

The bishop as pastor

Let us consider again the first of the two pictures. The Shepherd-God has his under-shepherds. The writer of Psalm 77, looking back over Israel's history, says to God, 'You guided your people like a flock, shepherded by Moses and Aaron' (77:20). Jesus himself is referred to as 'the great Shepherd of the sheep' (Hebrews 13:20). When a bishop is consecrated, the Archbishop prays, 'Enable him as a true shepherd to feed and govern your flock.' The most eloquent part of a bishop's regalia is the pastoral staff which he carries in his hand. It is a constant reminder to him that he goes to his work not as a managing director, not as an organizer, not as a chairman of committees, but as a pastor, a shepherd whose supreme task is to guide the people, to guard them, and to fulfil the costly ministry which he shares with the great Shepherd of the sheep. There is a significant passage in Peter Hebblethwaite's *Life of Paul VI* in which he describes the Pope's desire to 'find a new type of bishop... less like top executives who can read a financial statement, more enabling pastors with enough theology to know what implementing the [Vatican] Council meant'.

When the Church of England commemorates St Matthias, chosen to be of the number of the Twelve in the place of the traitor Judas, it prays, 'Preserve your Church from false apostles, and by the ministry of faithful pastors and teachers, keep us steadfast in your truth' (*Alternative Service Book 1980*).

TO PONDER

In our cathedrals, the Bishop's chair is not a throne. It is his seat, there to remind us that, in past centuries, a teacher sat to teach while his students stood to learn. The Bishop is a teacher, a guardian of the Faith.

FESTIVAL TIME

The psalm opens noisily. It is festival time, and the worshippers are called not only to join in song (v. 1) but to use any instrument they can lay hands on—drum, lyre, harp (v. 2), ram's horn (v. 3)—when the moon is new or when it is at the full (v. 3). (See also the comment on Psalm 95.)

Then a hush comes over the assembly—someone is speaking with a prophetic word, unfamiliar to most of the people (v. 5b), and the whole emphasis of the psalm changes—'*Listen*, my people... O that you would *listen* to me, Israel' (v. 8). The tragedy of the nation is that its people would not listen (v. 11). But still there is hope for the future, if, and only if, God's people will listen to him (v. 13).

The heart of faith

Ask any religious Jew today what is the very heart of his faith, and he will reply by quoting Deuteronomy 6:4, 5: 'Hear, Israel: the Lord is our God, the Lord our one God; and you must love the Lord your God with all your heart and with all your soul and with all your strength.' Indeed, Jesus, when asked by one of the scribes which was the first of all the commandments, replied by quoting these verses. They are called the *Shema*, which is the Hebrew word that opens the verses. It means 'hear, listen, attend'. The context of these verses is of immense importance—the oneness of God, our God; and love for that God with every fibre of the human being. This is not the place to elaborate these words. But I would suggest that the most important part of the *Shema* is the opening word: *Listen*. These great theological truths are of no avail unless they are taken on board, unless there is an attentive mind, a listening ear, a responsive heart. Listen!

In the context of this psalm, it is as if the writer is saying to the worshippers: there is room for music, for song, for the noise of voices and instruments (vv. 1–3), for exuberance. But now—cease from it all. Let there be silence. Or, as the writer of Psalm 95 puts it, 'If only you would listen to him now!' (95:7b).

What has this to say to us in terms of the worship of the church which we attend? Is the congregation being taught to be a listening body—before the service begins and at points during its course (for example, after the lessons, and after the sermon, and during the intercessions). The Lord's message here is a plea to his people to listen—'If my people would but listen to me' (v. 13)—a listening that would issue in obedience, deliverance and blessing: 'Israel would be fed with the finest flour and satisfied with honey from the rocks' (v. 16).

It was for lack of such listening that Israel ran into disaster (vv. 11ff.). Are we ready to listen to that lesson from history? (See Psalm 95:7b–11.)

TO PONDER

When you cried to me in distress, I rescued you;
I answered you from the thunder cloud.
(Psalm 81:7)

PSALM 82

The SUPREME JUDGE

God is depicted in this psalm as presiding over a court of super-human beings, superhuman in the esteem of ordinary people, but coming under God's rebuke and judgment. There is a similar concept in Psalm 89:5–7 ('the court of heaven', 'the council of the angels') and, less dramatically, in Job 2:1–6.

The speech of the presiding Judge of the judges occupies the major part of the psalm (vv. 2–4 and 6–7). He accuses his people of injustice, and of failure to support the underdog and rescue the weak from the clutches of the powerful (vv. 2–4). He passes sentence on them—they shall die like any mortal, 'fall as any prince does' (v. 7). God's concern for the oppressed is a favourite theme of the psalmists (see, especially, Psalm 146) and of the prophets: religious ritual divorced from social concern is blasphemy (see, for example, Isaiah 1:10–17). There is a strong element of mockery, of bitter irony, in this psalm. The writer of Psalm 115 ridicules gods made with mouths which cannot speak, eyes which cannot see, ears which cannot hear, and so on—mere blocks of silver and gold. Worst of all, their makers and their followers come to share the futile nature of the gods themselves (115:4–8). Isaiah spells out the folly of such religiosity in a scathing passage (Isaiah 44:9–20), and it is hard to beat the story in which the prophet Elijah mocks the prophets of Baal for their futile prayer to a god who may be deep in thought, or perchance has gone to the lavatory, or perhaps just nodded off (1 Kings 18:27)! What intelligent person would worship such a god as that? (Have you ever seen on the television the excitement of the worshippers of Mammon when their god has answered their cries and granted them an award in the National Lottery?) It is all so ephemeral, so passing, so transitory. As another psalmist put it, 'What is of little worth wins general esteem' (Psalm 12:8).

Shaken to the foundations

'Meanwhile earth's foundations are all giving way' (v. 5b). Are they so blind that they cannot see that if you play fast and loose with the moral order, disaster must follow as certainly as night follows day? If the basic unity of the family is allowed to crumble; if 'anything goes' in the sphere of sexual relationships; if 'thou shalt not be found out' is exchanged for 'thou shalt not covet' or 'thou shalt not steal' in the world of business; if, in short, as the psalmist says, 'earth's foundations are all giving way', what hope is there for humankind but the road of penitence and birth from above? As Jesus explained to Nicodemus, 'Flesh can give birth only to flesh; it is spirit that gives birth to spirit... You must all be born again' (John 3:6, 7).

Verse 8: the irony ends. The protest ceases. The psalmist turns—where else can he turn?—to God, the Judge; immortal, invisible, God only wise; the Creator God, to whom 'coasts and islands weigh as light as specks of dust' (Isaiah 40:15). 'God, arise and judge the earth, for all the nations are yours'—it is a great asseveration; it is a cry arising from near-despair to hope in the living God.

TO PONDER

*'It is all so ephemeral, so passing, so transitory,' we said, referring
to what T.S. Eliot calls the world of the 'hollow men'. It will end,
'not with a bang but a whimper'. Jim Cotter puts it well in his
comment, headed 'The Idle Promise of Idols', on Psalm 82:*

> *They seem to be as gods,*
> *those who promise utopias,*
> *Fickle as a crowd we gawp,*
> *cheering the latest idolatry;*
> *Romantic illusions of singers.*
> *false pledges of politicians,*
> *slippery words of gurus,*
> *sleek suits of the televangelists.*

From *By Stony Paths*, Cairns Publications, 1991

WARRING NATIONS

The best way to understand this psalm would be to spend a little time with a map of the Middle East. A general survey would make clear the immense importance, militarily and commercially, of the little strip which we call the Land of Israel. Those at the head of the great powers—Egypt, Assyria, Rome, to mention only three—looked with covetous eyes on a land whose area was small but whose territory was strategically vital to their interests.

Then we should look at a map of Israel in the time of the Judges, and note the little nations close to Israel which were always snapping at its heels and at war with its leaders. Then we should read Judges 4—8 to understand the references to Israel's victories over such local foes; 'battles long ago' they may have been, but they were part of the warp and woof of which Israel's history was being made. This background reading will pay us good dividends as we come to understand the nations, great and small, who said, 'Let us wipe them out as a nation... let the name of Israel be remembered no more' (v. 4); 'We will seize for ourselves the territory of God's people' (v. 12).

Covetousness on the part of the surrounding nations issued in war to obtain territory; fear and war on the part of Israel issued in hatred of the oppressors, a hatred vividly expressed in verses 13–17. (See also Psalm 60.)

This is no place to comment on the present situation in the Middle East, fraught as it is with conflict over territorial rights, which itself might lead to an explosion of war among the nations. But history and geography have always combined to make this area a tinderbox of national, racial and tribal interest. What we must not be tempted to do is to use those historic tensions to fuel the evil of anti-Semitism, an evil going back to the earliest days of the Christian religion and which even yet rears its ugly head today.

Centuries of prejudice

The fact of the Diaspora, the dispersion of the Jewish people outside Israel, has been a blessing to humanity because of the brilliance of the contribution which Jews have made wherever they have spread. But again and again their presence has been met by antipathy on the part of their Gentile neighbours, and the Jews have been the target of discrimination and hatred. This reached its awful climax in the Holocaust and the attempt at genocide on the part of the Nazis. But suspicion of and antipathy to Jews has been manifested in a thousand more subtle ways—anti-Semitism has been like an underground fire which erupts often where it is least expected. The work of the International Council of Christians and Jews, and other similar agencies, is doing much to alert us to the danger of such eruptions, and, more positively, through education and publications, is leading to mutual understanding. For the ignorance on the part of Christians of things Jewish, and on the part of Jews of the Christian faith, is still profound, and the task of counteracting such ignorance is huge. In fact, it sometimes seems as if only a small start has been made.

TO PONDER

1. As a Christian, I am indebted to the Jewish religion and tradition. Wherein does that debt mainly consist?

2. Have I ever been to a synagogue, or attended a Jewish service? Have I a Jewish friend who would take me to a Jewish service?

TO PRAY

Let us pray for God's ancient people, the Jews,
the first to hear his word—
for greater understanding between Christian and Jew,
for the removal of our blindness and bitterness of heart,
that God will grant us grace to be faithful to his covenant
and to grow in the love of his name.

May the Christ who once reconciled Jew and Gentile, slave and freeman into one body, continue to break down the walls which divide us.

SHEER JOY

This is a psalm of sheer joy—a welcome change after the sorrows sketched in some of the psalms which precede it! It is a pilgrim's poem, written with the freedom of the poet and the exhilaration which comes from joyful worship. At long last, the journey to Jerusalem is over. Solomon's temple, with all its gleaming magnificence, comes in sight. Every step brings him closer to the 'courts of the Lord's temple' (v. 2), 'your dwelling-place' (v. 1), 'your house' (v. 4). There is the Ark, that symbol of God's presence and nearness. Of course he cannot penetrate to the Holy of Holies, where the Ark is kept, for only the high priest can do so, and that only once a year. But to spend even one day in God's courts is better than a thousand in his own home (v. 10). Perhaps he casts a covetous eye on 'those who *dwell* in your house', and who are able to share in the organized services of praise in the temple (v. 4).

The pilgrim's long trek is over. Looking back, it was worth every step. The heat of the waterless valley was fierce; looking back, he sees it full of springs and pools (v. 6). God had cared for him, and—a touch of humour here!—he feels like a sparrow which, after flying hither and thither in search of a place of safety for its young, finds it 'beside your altar, Lord of Hosts, my King and God' (v. 3). He would have delighted in the saying of Jesus: 'Are not two sparrows sold for a penny? Yet without your Father's knowledge not one of them can fall to the ground... You are worth more than any number of sparrows' (Matthew 10:29, 31).

On the road home

The picture of God's people as pilgrims on the road to their permanent home is a powerful one. Peter wrote to 'the scattered people of God now living as aliens in' various places in Asia Minor (1 Peter 1:1). Their true home was in heaven. 'For here we have no lasting city, but we are seekers after the city which is to come' (Hebrews 13:14). A pilgrim travels light, stripped of things which would hinder his progress. A pilgrim is prepared for the unexpected—a new day will bring new challenges and opportunities. A pilgrim makes the most of his daily rations of food—prayer, work, sacrament are there to sustain him. Yes, Christians are a pilgrim people—*en route*.

TO PONDER

1. A phrase: What does it mean to 'dwell in God's house' (v. 4)?

> *It is recorded of Anna that 'she never left the temple, but worshipped night and day with fasting and prayer' (Luke 2:37). She could be said to have 'dwelt in' the house of the Lord. But that is not possible for most of us. Would Psalms 23:6 and 27:4 help us to answer the question?*

2. A poem, written by Lord Hailsham, wistful but not without hope, for the day is coming when the sparrow will soar like a lark:

> *Father, before the sparrow's earthly flight*
> *Ends in the darkness of a winter's night;*
> *Father, without whose word no sparrow falls,*
> *Hear this, thy weary sparrow, when he calls.*
> *Mercy, not justice, is his contrite prayer,*
> *Cancel his guilt and drive away despair;*
> *Speak but the word, and make his spirit whole,*
> *Cleanse the dark places of his heart and soul.*
> *Speak but the word, and set his spirit free;*
> *Mercy, not justice, still his constant plea.*
> *So shall thy sparrow, crumpled wings restored,*
> *Soar like a lark, and glorify his Lord.*

'The Sparrow's Prayer',
from Robert Llewelyn's *Memories and Reflections*, p. 240

LOVING *the* NATION

The man who wrote this psalm had a deep love and concern for his own people, the nation of which he was a part. He was a true patriot.

There is a false patriotism and there is a true one. The false patriot proclaims: '*My country right or wrong*'. He is concerned about its financial welfare, its status among other nations, its prosperity, in temporal terms only. He does not mind if its leaders are 'economical with the truth'. Morals do not concern him. The destruction of the family as we have known it over the centuries does not worry him. He is a hedonist, if that word can be used in a national and not only a personal sense. The idea of men and women as trustees with God in the ongoing creation of the world is foreign to him.

The true patriot, on the other hand, cares deeply for the world in which he lives, and particularly for the nation of which he is a part. He longs for its peace (vv. 8, 10, 13) in the biblical sense of that word (*shalom*). Peace has social dimensions to it—it has to do with righteousness and judgment and the actions of public officials. 'Justice and peace have *embraced*': truly, the two must go together, for without justice there is no true peace. It has to do with relationships and with people living in tranquillity. It has to do with relationship with God who creates peace. It is a wide-ranging concept—well-being national and personal under the smile of God. The pursuit of peace is likely to be very costly, for often it can only be attained through battle with such evils as colour-bar, denial of women's rights, injustice in the law-courts.

Bishop Trevor Huddleston loved South Africa and its people with a deep love. It was a costly love. In the words of the *Times* obituary (21 April 1998): 'He fought for better conditions for the Africans whom he knew and loved, he fought police oppression and hooliganism, he strove to get better living and employment conditions, he challenged the pass laws, he addressed political meetings and was at one point within an ace of being flung into prison...'. Peace, in other words, comes with a price.

Eternal vigilance

The psalm opens on a happy note. The people have been forgiven; God's anger is withdrawn (vv. 1–3), but there is always the possibility of going 'back to foolish ways' (v. 8). We can never rest secure about the continuance of 'peace'. 'The condition upon which God hath given liberty to man is eternal vigilance' (J.P. Curran). The writer of the letter to the Hebrews warns us, 'We are bound to pay all the more heed to what we have been told, for fear of drifting from our course' (Hebrews 2:1).

The psalmist is at his listening-post—'Let me hear the words of God the Lord' (v. 8). He longs that 'glory may dwell in our land' (v. 9). What is the soil in which such 'glory' will flourish? He has no doubt about the answer. Watch his vocabulary: 'worship' (v. 9); 'love and faithfulness; justice and peace' (v. 10); 'faithfulness and justice' (v. 11); 'justice and peace' (v. 13). The repetition seems to underline what is essential. These are the qualities that distinguish the kingdom of God, the place where he is sovereign.

PRAYER

The truest patriot is the person who prays for the peace of his country, the land of his birth or of his adoption. 'Pray for the peace of Jerusalem' (Psalm 122:6). Pray, now, for the peace of Britain—Canada—Uganda... wherever you live. Pray for peace in its fullest sense—for glory in our land.

PSALM 86

KEEPING *the* FAITH

It is not easy to keep the faith and to bear our witness to God when we are surrounded by people who have no faith or who actively oppose those who have. The atmosphere is like a damp fog which penetrates the body and oppresses the mind.

The Jews were surrounded by nations who worshipped gods other than Yahweh, the God of Israel. The temptation to give in to the claims of polytheism, to worship other gods, to succumb to the prevalent manner of life which they saw surrounding them, was constant.

There were various ways of meeting the opposition. One way was by the use of satire. As we have seen, the writer of Isaiah 44:9–20 mocks those who manufacture wooden images. In a passage of biting satire, he describes a man who picks out in the forest an ilex or an oak. He fells it. Some of it he uses to cook his meal or to keep himself warm—'Good! I can feel the heat as I watch the flames,' he says. What is left of the tree he chops up and makes into a god to which he says: 'Save me; for you are my god.' How can an intelligent man be so silly?

The writer of this psalm approaches the problem not with satire, but with humility: 'I am oppressed and poor... Lord, listen to my prayer and hear my pleading' (vv. 1, 6). He addresses God himself in a prayer which is partly petition and partly a witness to what he is finding in his worship of the one God. It is a declaration of the greatness and the goodness of God, and a prayer to One who is quite clearly the joy of his life. He is a God who, unlike the gods of his neighbours, answers prayer (v. 7), who is 'kind and forgiving, full of love towards all who cry to' him (v. 5), who is great and whose 'works are wonderful' (v. 10).

There is a lively relationship between the psalmist and his God. He wants to worship him 'with undivided heart', to praise him with all his heart (vv. 11 and 12). To do so is not only to fulfil a duty but to find joy in it. He addresses God as 'compassionate and gracious, long-suffering, ever faithful and true' (v. 15).

Just a beginner

Face to face with a God like that, the psalmist can only pray, 'Lord, teach me your way, that I may walk in your truth' (v. 11). He is only a beginner. However long his discipleship has been, he needs to go to school. He has just dipped his toes in the ocean of God's love. He must go on learning and exploring, till he can learn to swim and to get out into the deep. He is engaged in a lifelong exploration into God. He wants to 'walk in your truth' (v. 11), for he is a pilgrim among a pilgrim people—and we know what that means (see Psalm 84). He ends by reaffirming that faith: 'For you, Lord, have been my help and comfort.'

LET US PRAY

Abiding is your love,
enduring is your patience,
everlasting are your truths,
eternal is your glory;
O God, you are God.

Jim Cotter, *By Stony Paths*, Cairns Publications, 1991

PSALM 87

The BELOVED CITY

If we spread out on the desk in front of us three or four versions of this psalm, we shall note how much one version differs from another. This points to two matters which we should bear in mind. The first is that the Hebrew text is very difficult, and it is more than probable that it has been damaged in the long years of its transmission from generation to generation. The second is that the psalm is a poem, and rhapsodic poems should not be read as if they were sober prose. The meaning of a poem by an author like T.S. Eliot does not lie on its surface. It is suggestive, and may convey a different nuance to different readers. That is a matter of no regret. It is of the very nature of poetry.

The opening three verses are a eulogy of Zion, 'the city the Lord founded' (v. 1), which 'he loves' above all other buildings (v. 2), the 'city of God', well spoken of (v. 3).

But its glory does not consist merely in its magnificent buildings. God's interest is in the people who visit it. God is the speaker in verse 4: he sees his city as the mother of the faithful of all the world, the great powers of Egypt (Rahab) and Babylon, and the little nations of Philistines and Tyrians and (even) of dark-skinned Nubians (no colour-bar with God!) But among them stand the 'natives' of Jerusalem, proud of their birthright: 'This one and that one were born there... this one was born there' (vv. 5, 6).

A great pilgrim festival

Arthur Weiser, in his commentary on the Psalms, sees the poet as standing in the temple of Jerusalem 'on the occasion of a great pilgrim-festival...'

> *People from all over the world pass by before the eyes of the singer. It is as if the whole world had arranged to meet in this place... However much they may differ from each other in language and appearance, they are all united in one faith, believing in the one God whom they jointly profess. The hymn which they sing (v. 7) impresses itself deeply on the poet's memory; for all of them the temple of Jerusalem is their home, though cradled in some remote country' (The Psalms: A Commentary, p. 580).*

52

There is a remarkable passage in the book of Zechariah (8:20–23) in which the prophet has the vision of a day when 'many peoples and mighty nations... of every language will take hold of the robe of one Jew and say: "Let us accompany you, for we have heard that God is with you."' So the ancient prophecy would be fulfilled that through God's people, Israel, all the world would be blessed (Genesis 12:2–3). That is Israel's supreme destiny.

Our psalmist sees God entering up his register of the peoples (v. 6), a vast variety of nations owing him allegiance. No wonder that the psalm ends with music and dancing—there is much to celebrate. 'The source of all good is in you' (v. 7).

PRAISE AND PRAYER

Glorious things of thee are spoken,
Zion, city of our God;
He whose word cannot be broken
formed thee for his own abode.
On the Rock of ages founded,
what can shake thy sure repose?
With salvation's walls surrounded,
thou mayst smile at all thy foes.

Saviour, since of Zion's city,
I through grace a member am,
Let the world deride or pity,
I will glory in thy name.
Fading is the worldling's pleasure,
all his boasted pomp and show:
Solid joys and lasting treasure
none but Zion's children know.

John Newton (1725–1807)

PSALM 88

DOWN *to the* PIT

I doubt whether in the whole of the Old Testament there is so detailed a description of the Hebrew view of what would happen after death as in this psalm. We do well to spare a moment to examine it. The psalmist paints the picture because he has been the victim of a near-fatal illness—he has been brought to 'the brink of Sheol' (v. 3).

Had he died, he says, he would have gone down to the abyss, beyond help, abandoned, forgotten by God, cut off from his care, 'plunged… into the darkest regions of the depths' (vv. 4–6). It is of no use to think that God will work wonders for anybody in Sheol, nor is the voice of praise to be heard there. No mention will be made of God's faithfulness in days gone by—Sheol is the land of oblivion (vv. 10–11). It is a dark and dismal description.

The psalmist's concept of the meaning of his own illness only makes things worse. He is convinced that God is furious with him—his onslaughts have overwhelmed him (vv. 7, 15–17). His friends have abandoned him, thinking that he is 'utterly loathsome' (vv. 8 and 18)—his only companion now is darkness. The only shaft of light in this psalm is that the writer still dares to pray and to call God 'my God' (v. 1).

If there is justification for the inclusion of this psalm in a psalter used by Christians—and I believe there is such justification—it is that it conveys to the reader the total contrast between the psalmist's picture of death and of God himself and that which is to be found within the Christian revelation. Listen to this: 'I looked and saw a vast throng, which no one could count, from all… nations and languages, standing before the throne and the Lamb' (Revelation 7:9).

Listen again: 'I am convinced that there is nothing in death or life… nothing in all creation that can separate us from the love of God in Christ Jesus our Lord' (Romans 8:38–39).

So we could go on. There is a hemisphere of difference between the two positions—of death and its aftermath, and of God and his relationship with us.

Christian living and dying

If the Christian doctrine of death, and of the God whom we shall meet after death, is true, its impact on Christian living and dying is immediate and powerful. True, there is a host of questions left unresolved—'At present we see only puzzling reflections in a mirror, but one day we shall see face to face' (1 Corinthians 13:12). 'We are now God's children; what we shall be has not yet been disclosed, but we know that when Christ appears we shall be like him, because we shall see him as he is.' That is a conviction which is cathartic—'Everyone who has grasped this hope makes himself pure' (1 John 3:2–3). It is the conviction of the resurrection-people of God. However, we read the words, they stand in stark contrast to the bleak persuasion of verses 10–12. The psalmist's honesty is impressive but, in ultimate terms, hopeless: 'Darkness is now my only companion' (v. 18). Thank God, therefore, for the Christian hope, that looks with confidence *beyond* the grave.

LET US PRAISE

Jesus lives! thy terrors now
can no more, O death, appal us;
Jesus lives! by this we know
thou, O grave, can'st not enthral us. Alleluia!

Jesus lives! for us he died;
then, alone to Jesus living,
Pure in heart may we abide,
glory to our Saviour giving. Alleluia!

C.F. Gellert (1715–69), trs. Frances E. Cox (1812–97)

Let us rejoice and exult,
and give glory and homage to our God.

PSALM 89

A PSALM *of* COVENANT

Let us suppose that we were in touch with someone who had some acquaintance with the literature of world religions, but who hitherto was not conversant with the basic literature of the Jewish and Christian faiths. He asks us, 'What sort of God shall I find in these books?' Our answer must necessarily be brief and expressed in simple language. I would venture to reply something like this: 'The God of the Bible is one who passionately longs to be in touch with his creation, to enter into relationship with his people, and who is prepared to take the initiative, however costly, in bringing this about. He is a God of love who keeps his word and looks for a response.' In saying this, I would be introducing him to the idea of 'covenant' which is a central concept in the Judeo-Christian scheme of things. 'I will be their God; they shall be my people.'

The concept of covenant is central to Psalm 89. It opens on a note of gratitude for God's faithfulness to his word; and verses 3 and 4, spoken by God himself, explain the nature of his covenant. This elicits from the psalmist a paean of thankfulness for two things: God's trustworthiness—he never goes back on his word—and his power (over Rahab the sea-monster in verse 10). The God who initiates his covenant with Israel has a throne founded on righteousness, justice, love and faithfulness—it is a good quartet!

Our psalmist has in mind one special aspect of God's covenant—it is his promise to David that his line, his throne, should endure. This is mentioned in verses 3 and 4, and taken up in considerable detail in verses 19–29. There is a note of intimacy, a Father-son relationship, which is remarkable here (vv. 26–27).

Embittered by chaos

A more sombre note is introduced in verses 30ff. It takes two to make a covenant, and there is the possibility that Israel will default. That would involve Israel in punishment, but God would never break his word (vv. 33–37). As Paul was to put it many years later, 'The gracious gifts of God and his calling are irrevocable' (Romans 11:29). 'All the promises of God have their Yes' in Christ (2 Corinthians 1:20). The covenant *principle* remained, but the content of the covenant had been transformed. As we are reminded every time we share in the Eucharist, a new covenant ratified by the blood of Christ has been made by God with his Church. Yet it is a covenant and God says, 'I shall not alter my covenant, nor alter what I have promised.'

The last section of our psalm takes on a tragic tone. The writer turns on God, charging God with renouncing the covenant he had made with his servant. God seems to be responsible for the disaster which has befallen his people—'*you* have... *you* have... *you* have...' (vv. 38–45). And how long will this kind of treatment be handed out—how long?—'Where are your former loving deeds, Lord?' (vv. 46–51). The psalmist, embittered by the chaos by which he is surrounded and sobered by the transitoriness of human existence, rages against God. He has many questions and much despair, yet, significantly, it is to *God* that he continues to look for answers!

LET US PRAISE

My song shall be always of the loving kindness of the Lord—
the love that sought us and found us,
the grace that made a covenant with us,
the patience that kept us when we were faithless,
the cost of the new covenant in Christ's blood.

My song shall be always of the loving kindness of the Lord.
Praise the Lord, my soul,
Evermore and Evermore.
Amen and Amen.

[Verse 52 is not a part of the psalm. It is a formal ascription of glory to God to mark the end of the third book of the Psalter (Psalms 73—89)]

As Time Goes By

Time is a very precious commodity. It slips by very quickly. When we were little, a year seemed like an age. When we get older we find ourselves saying 'I don't know where the time has gone.' One thing about time of which we can be sure—it is irrevocable!

The brevity of life impressed our psalmist deeply. He uses various metaphors to describe it. We humans are like grass, quickly shooting up, as quickly drooping and withering (vv. 5 and 6). Death comes like sleep (v. 5), like a murmur or a sigh (v. 9). If we make seventy, that's all we can expect, and if eighty, we cannot hope for much besides toil and sorrow (v. 10). (Modern science has enabled us to put up the score by a decade or so, but we take the psalmist's point.) All this depresses the writer.

But for him there is something even more depressing. It is his concept of a God who is angry with him—he is terrified by his wrath (v. 7), he feels the power of his anger (v. 11). Wherein does the attitude of the Christian differ from the psalmist's?

We share his concept of the brevity, the transitoriness, of human existence. We welcome his emphasis on the 'everlastingness' of God (v. 2). (The writer of Hebrews 1:10ff. quotes Psalm 102:25–27 to make the same point.) We note the contrast of the passing with the permanent. We recall Paul's insistence on the 'three things that last for ever: faith, hope, and love' (1 Corinthians 13:13). These are what our forebears called 'the eternal verities'.

God's rescue plan

But what about the frowning God under whose wrath the psalmist passes his days (v. 9)? Listen to Paul: 'Now that we have been justified through faith, we are at peace with God through our Lord Jesus Christ… and we exult in the hope of the divine glory that is to be ours' (Romans 5:1, 2). God 'rescued us from the domain of darkness and brought us into the kingdom of his dear Son…' (Colossians 1:13). If this means anything, it means that the Christian can look up into the face of God and laugh for joy. 'Now your life lies hidden with Christ in God. When Christ, who is our life, is revealed, then you too will be revealed with him in glory' (Colossians 3:3–4).

Our psalmist has little idea of 'the life of the world to come'. But he has hope for his children, and he prays for them (v. 16). In them, perhaps, he sees the hint of a brighter future. They may come to see 'the saving acts of the Lord', sharing his faith in the one who 'has been our refuge throughout all generations'.

PRAYER

Let us pray for discernment to perceive the difference between the things that are permanent and those that are passing. (A reading of Wisdom 4 and 5 [The Apocrypha] would be of interest.)

Let us pray that we 'may so pass through things temporal, that we finally lose not the things eternal'.

O God of our ancestors, God of our people,
before whose face the human generations pass away;
We thank you that in you we are kept safe for ever,
and that the broken fragments of our history are gathered up
in the redeeming act of your dear Son,
remembered in the holy sacrament of bread and wine.
Help us to walk daily in the Communion of Saints,
declaring our faith in the forgiveness of sins
and the resurrection of the body.
Now send us out in the power of your Holy Spirit,
to live and work to your praise and glory.

Kenyan rite of Eucharist

ANGELS *on* DUTY

Let us be honest in reading this psalm. The writer is facing the problem of disasters when they menace the godly and when they menace the ungodly. To put it in a nutshell, he says that the righteous will be sheltered by God's overshadowing power—'A thousand may fall at your side, ten thousand close at hand, but you it will not touch' (vv. 7 and 10 etc.)—it is the wicked who will face retribution (v. 8). But is the psalmist facing the facts of life and experience? Is not his solution to the problem too facile, too easy? For example, in a war when bullets are raining down on the troops, God does not appear to deflect bullets from the godly while allowing them to find their target on the ungodly. The same applies in an air crash, or in an earthquake, or in a car crash. We may quote examples of miraculous escapes—and there are plenty of such instances available—but even in those cases there appears to be no divine favouring of the righteous! Where were the angels on duty when those disasters occurred? (v. 11) This, of course, is the passage quoted by the Tempter to Jesus as he urged him to throw himself from the pinnacle of the temple, and demonstrate God's power in his life (Matthew 4:5–7). The response of Jesus was that we should not 'put the Lord to the test'. Angelic protection should never be taken for granted!

We must remember that the psalmist had little, if any, concept of a life after death such as is evident in the pages of the New Testament. The author of the book of Wisdom, writing later than our psalmist, faces the problem posed by the death of a person who is still young; he has something worthwhile to say about it: 'But the just person, even one who dies an untimely death, will be at rest. It is not length of life and number of years which bring the honour due to age; if people have understanding, they have grey hairs enough, and an unblemished life is the true ripeness of age' (Wisdom 4:7–9). But the Christian with his resurrection hope in Christ has brighter prospects than psalmist or Wisdom-writer. There is a time coming (when time ceases to be!) when evil has been finally defeated and 'there shall be an end to death, and to mourning and crying and pain, for the old order has passed away' (Revelation 21:4). This does not solve our problem—our eyes are often blinded with tears—but it eases it.

Learning trust

Further, there is a depth of meaning in such phrases as 'living in the shelter of the Most High' and 'lodging under the shadow of the Almighty' (v. 1). That speaks of a life lived in communion with God which leads us to trust when we cannot see. As we learn that truth, we can walk with firmer step and sleep with less troubled mind. God has a gift of serenity for those who know that 'his love holds fast to me' (v. 14). Henri Nouwen, commenting on Rembrandt's picture of the father welcoming his prodigal son, notes the father's great red cloak:

> With its warm colour and its arch-like shape, it offers a welcome place where it is good to be... As I went on gazing at the red cloak the image of the sheltering wings of the mother bird came strongly to me. Every time I look at the... wings-like cloak in Rembrandt's painting I sense the motherly quality of God's love and my heart begins to sing in words inspired by the Psalmist: 'You who dwell in the shelter of the Most High and abide in the shade of the Almighty—say to your God: My refuge, my stronghold, my God in whom I trust! ... You covered me with your pinions and under your wings I shall find refuge.'
>
> (H. Nouwen, *The Return of the Prodigal Son*, pp. 99–100)

In short, Christianity does not provide an escape from disaster but it does offer hope, strength, and freedom from bitterness.

A QUESTION

How seriously do you take the Motherhood of God?

ALONE *with* HIS GOD

Many of the psalms are intended for people worshipping on great occasions in the temple. There are choirs and instrumental accompaniment. Not so this psalm. Here I see a man alone with his God. The caption reads, 'A psalm: a song: for the sabbath day'. Why only 'for the sabbath day'? This might equally well be a description of a man's pattern of daily worship, meditation, thanksgiving. Every day he addresses himself to this task. It is his recipe for a healthy, holy life. He reckons it to be a poor day which does not begin in this way. Here he sits; it helps him to have a harp (v. 3), a lyre (a guitar?) to accompany his faltering words. As he plucks its strings, his spirits rise in adoration.

The emphasis is on thanksgiving. He is a grateful man. How good God has been! Gratitude unfreezes him. He looks back over the history of his people, over his own life. God has made himself known through his acts, his deeds (vv. 4, 5), his deep thoughts of love. 'I alone know my purpose for you, says the Lord: well-being and not misfortune' (Jeremiah 29:11). 'Always be joyful... give thanks whatever happens' (1 Thessalonians 5:16, 18). The writer of Psalm 139 elaborates the thought-life of God, as we shall see. God's acts, God's thoughts, are the basis of the psalmist's thanks.

The stupidity of evil-doers

Verse 6: the music stops. A cloud passes over the scene. The psalmist's mind turns to a consideration of the sheer stupidity of evil-doers. How foolish they are! Will they never learn that evil has within it the seeds of destruction and decay? The history of his own nation abounds with illustrations. Had he been able to look down the corridors of later history, he would have noted that Paul referred to the governing powers of the great Roman empire as being 'already in decline' (1 Corinthians 2:6). Some 350 years later, the city of Rome having been sacked in 410, Augustine of Hippo wrote of another city, the City of God, which would never crumble. Early in the sixteenth century, Luther was to write of another tyranny which 'for all their craft and force, one moment will not linger... These things shall vanish all: The City of God remaineth.'

In our own day, we have seen the tyrants come and go—Mussolini, Hitler, Idi Amin, Pol Pot... The tyrants are blind; they cannot read the lessons of history—they 'perish', they are 'scattered' (v. 9).

Verse 10: the psalmist turns from the general to the particular, from God's 'enemies' to himself. He uses a variety of illustrations—the wild ox's horns, oil (v. 10), trees (vv. 12–14), rock (v. 15). A wild ox uses his horns to protect his body in case of assault by another beast—whether by getting in first with his own horns, or by so inter-locking them with those of his opponent that he can exhaust him. Humans use bullet-proof jackets! God's 'enemies' will perish, but the believer enjoys his favour ('oil') and protection ('horns').

Oil (v. 10, cf. Psalm 23:5) was ceremonially used when a king was anointed (see, for example, 1 Samuel 10:1). Messiah (Hebrew) and Christ (Greek) simply mean 'one who is anointed'. Perhaps our writer has in mind some high office to which he has attained. But oil was also commonly used for cleansing (when water was scarce), and for rubbing in to ease arthritic pain, to soothe, to further suppleness and flexibility. It is a fruitful picture for a Christian disciple. We all have hang-ups and stand in need of openness and flexibility of mind; we have our hurts, resulting from the 'slings and arrows of outrageous fortune', from which we need release.

Trees (vv. 12–14)—palm, cedar, fruit trees, luxuriant, wide-spread-ing—speak of shelter for oneself and for others in time of searing heat or pouring rain. They speak of usefulness, in terms of carpentry and furnishing. They speak of fruit-bearing.

Was it an old man who wrote verses 13 and 14? Is this an auto-biographical touch of a man who has grown old gracefully, but still is useful in his later years, bearing the marks of the Spirit's harvest (Galatians 5:22–23), not rusting but ripening? Everything depends on your roots—his were planted 'in the house of the Lord... in the courts of our God' (v. 13).

PRAISE

There are three things that last for ever: faith, hope, and love.
(1 Corinthians 13:13)

Anoint me, Lord, richly with the oil of your loving spirit.

MEDITATING *on* GOD

I see in the writer of this psalm a man who simply meditates on God. He is content to ask for nothing. Unlike many other psalmists, he complains about nothing. Intercession is not his concern. Whatever he does at other times when he comes into God's presence, now he wants only to meditate on God, and especially on his greatness. He devotes himself to this alone, sometimes addressing God (vv. 2, 5), sometimes allowing us to share his thoughts with him.

How can he conceive of the majesty of God, how describe his greatness? Human language is of little use, but he has no other means of expressing what is on his mind. He calls on two pictures to help him: the picture of the king, and the picture of the sea.

The king (v. 1). It is difficult for us who live in the modern world to conceive of what kingship conveyed in old days. Perhaps our grandparents or great-grandparents found that easier than we do. They knew what Queen Victoria meant—that little woman who reigned over those large parts of the world which were painted red in their school atlases, having immense authority over the vast millions of her subjects. Today, across the world, the idea of kingship has been tarnished by the atrocities of many who have occupied the thrones of their countries. And the junction of kingship and democracy has been—and is—a tricky one. But speak the word 'king' to a person living at the time of our psalmist, and he could see in the person of David enough marks of power, dignity, and care to make him pray for a Messiah with similar marks. Kingship and nobility went hand in hand.

Power and purity

The sea (v. 3). Jews did not like the sea. The great Mediterranean spoke of the danger of the unknown. Those few who set sail on it in their frail ships knew all too well of its treachery and its menace. The writer of the book of Revelation assures his readers that, in the new heaven and the new earth of his vision, 'there was no longer any sea' (Revelation 21:1).

And yet, our psalmist had stood and watched the crashing breakers as the tide came in. Frightening it might be for landlubbers like himself. But there was power in those waves, and purity in the waters that seemed to consume earth's rubbish and uncleanness. Power and purity—he must grant them that. With awe, he saw in the waves the marks of their Maker. 'Mightier than the sound of great waters, mightier than the breakers of the sea, mightier on high is the Lord' (v. 4).

Further, this God is not only a God of ineffable majesty. He is a God concerned with law and order in his creation and among his creatures. He has made his mind and will known by the 'decrees' which he has given (v. 5). Of this the sheer beauty of God's 'house', the temple (v. 5), gives at least some hint.

'Throughout the ages': it is a fitting note on which to end the psalm. In the light of God's eternity and human transience, we can only bow in wonder.

TO PONDER

F.W. Faber (1814–63) senses the psalmist's approach in his hymn:

> *My God, how wonderful thou art,*
> *Thy majesty how bright,*
> *How beautiful thy mercy-seat,*
> *In depths of burning light...*
> *How wonderful, how beautiful,*
> *The sight of thee must be,*
> *Thine endless wisdom, boundless power,*
> *And aweful purity!*

ARROGANCE & HUMILITY

The keynote of this psalm is in verse 2. The theme is arrogance, the pride of nations and individuals to whom God is an irrelevance. He can be banished from their reckoning. The very idea of a God, just and active in history, is outworn. Life can be managed without him. 'I am the master of my fate, I am the captain of my soul.'

The social results from such 'bluster, boasting and bragging' (v. 4) are palpably clear. People don't count. The defenceless, the widows, the fatherless, get crushed (vv. 5, 6).

Our psalmist rounds on the folly and stupidity of those who hold such views and pursue such policies without acknowledging that God knows their thoughts (vv. 8ff.). By way of contrast, he sketches the happiness of those humble enough to be instructed and taught by God (v. 12), and hints at the day which will come when 'justice will be joined to right' and the upright will be vindicated (vv. 12–15). He adds a word of witness to the help he himself has found in God in days when his feet were slipping (vv. 17ff.)—the Lord has been his 'strong tower', his 'rock and refuge' (v. 22).

In this century alone, we have watched the rise and fall of two great godless regimes—Communism with its gulags and Nazism with its concentration camps. These false philosophies have led to the deaths of hundreds of millions of defenceless victims, crushed under the heels of tyrants. 'The Lord knows that the thoughts of' such men 'are but a puff of wind' (v. 11)—Stalin has perished, the Berlin wall has crumbled.

Beware self-righteousness

But before we become self-righteous in our condemnation of communists and Nazis and before we gloat over their fall, we might well ask what God must think of other regimes which, for example, spend vast sums of public money in the production of sophisticated armoury when millions of people are dying for lack of food and hygiene. Has God's world gone mad? Will the day come, sooner or later, when the thoughts of the present world-powers are seen to be 'but a puff of wind'? (v. 11). These are hard questions, but they demand consideration. Must not a broken-hearted God cry out, as his Son did when surrounded by faithless disciples: 'What an unbelieving and perverse generation! How long shall I be with you and endure you?' (Luke 9:41).

LET US PONDER

Human pride and earthly glory,
Sword and cross betray our trust;
What with care and toil we fashion,
Tower and temple, fall to dust.
But God's power,
Hour by hour,
Is my temple and my tower.

LET US PRAISE

Still from man to God eternal
Sacrifice of praise be done,
High above all praises praising
For the gift of Christ his Son.
Christ doth call
One and all;
Ye who follow shall not fall.

Robert Bridges (1844–1930),
based on Joachim Neander (1650–80)

PSALM 95

CALL *to* CELEBRATE

Many psalmists invite their readers to enter with them into their experiences of sorrow and tragedy—they expose their griefs to God and to their fellows. It is also true that many psalms are invitations to join in the writers' joys. They are calls to celebrate with singing and, often, with all the music that can be mustered. For example, the writer of Psalm 35 cannot contain his joy. 'I shall rejoice in the Lord and delight in his salvation. My whole frame cries out, "Lord, who is there like you?"' (35:9–10). As the psalm (35) draws to a close, he bids his readers 'shout for joy, let them cry continually, "All glory to the Lord"' (35:27).

The writer of Psalm 95 has a congregation in mind, a group of worshippers going up together to the temple, probably for one of the great Jewish festivals. 'Come,' says a leader in the crowd, 'come! Let us raise a joyful song to the Lord, a shout of triumph to the rock of our salvation' (v. 1). Somebody strikes up; there is music and singing and strumming and laughter. There is noise in plenty as they reach the temple gates. 'Enter in!' says a voice from within the temple as the gates swing open. A hush comes over the assembly. 'Enter in! Let us bow down in worship, let us kneel before the Lord' (v. 6), our Creator-God, our Shepherd-God (v. 7). It is time to cease making noise, and to listen (v. 7b), to think back over history, to learn by past sinfulness not once again to be stubborn (vv. 8ff.). The sin of Meribah and Massah, putting God to the test, is ever lurking behind us.

Joy uninhibited

There is something almost boisterous about the opening verses of this psalm, something hilarious, joy uninhibited. These pilgrims are enjoying their God. Why shouldn't they? Family life is to be enjoyed. I have enjoyed my daughters at the various stages of their development, from their first dependence as infants to the mature development of later years. And I would like to think that they have enjoyed me! Joy in one another is at the heart of happy family life. If this is true on the human level, should it not also be true in the inter-relationship of our Father-God with his children? We should enjoy God, as we believe he enjoys us.

This is to put paid, once and for all, to a sour-faced religion. Christianity is celebration. We celebrate the resurrection. We celebrate the Eucharist—the very word means thanksgiving. We celebrate the gospel of release.

Before you leave this psalm, re-read the fifteenth chapter of Luke. 'Rejoice with me! I have found my lost sheep,' says the shepherd (v. 6). 'Rejoice with me! I have found the coin that I lost,' says the woman who mislaid a piece of her jewellery (v. 9). 'How could we fail to celebrate this happy day?' says the father of the boy who at last had come home. 'He was dead and has come back to life; he was lost and has been found' (v. 32). Let's have a party! Music, dancing, lots to eat and drink! And remember that when Jesus sought to depict the Reign of God, it was often in terms of a banquet, a wedding feast (for example, Luke 14:16ff.). 'Happy,' says the writer of Revelation, 'happy are those who are invited to the wedding banquet of the Lamb' (Revelation 19:9). Such joy in God is singularly independent of circumstances.

Of course, the warning remains. The joy is always conditional on obedience. The very people God chose and had loved could still go astray, and fail to find the sabbath rest, the joy of the Lord (vv. 7b–11).

TO NOTE

Under the very shadow of the cross, Jesus said to his disciples:
'I have spoken thus to you, so that my joy may be in you, and your
joy complete' (John 15:11).

SUMMONS *to* WORSHIP

This psalm is a summons to worship, as indeed Psalm 95 is also: 'Let us bow down in worship, let us kneel before the Lord who made us, for he is our God' (Psalm 95:6, 7). It is a summons to adoration. William Temple defined worship as 'the submission of all our nature to God... and all of this [is] gathered up in adoration, the most selfless emotion of which our nature is capable and therefore the chief remedy for that self-centredness which is our original sin and the source of all actual sin' (*Readings in St John's Gospel*). Adoration is an admission of God's greatness and our littleness. It is at the very heart of prayer.

Jesus is recorded as rebuffing the devil's invitation to him to fall down and worship him with a quotation from Deuteronomy 6:13: 'You shall do homage to the Lord your God and worship him alone' (Matthew 4:10).

Posture in worship does matter. We have noted the psalmist's 'Let us kneel' (95:6). Paul 'kneels in prayer to the Father' (Ephesians 3:14). The heavenly creatures surrounding God's throne in the Seer's vision in the book of Revelation 'prostrate themselves in worship' (4:10 and 5:14). There is less kneeling in public worship than there used to be. Is that a thing too trivial to mention here? I think not. To stand to attention while praying, or to kneel to express the reverence due to God is at once an antidote to sloppiness and a tribute to the almightiness of God. 'Obeisance,' my dictionary reminds me, 'is an attitude of deference or homage'. The opening verses of this psalm breathe 'worship'—'day by day proclaim his victory'.

Lifting up holy hands

These miracles of creation which are our bodies can be the means by which we acknowledge the 'otherness' of God. We lift up holy hands; we kneel to pray. Our bodies have a language of their own in worship, playing their part in a paean of praise which echoes the language of nature itself—heavens, sea, fields, trees of the forest all praising their Creator's name (vv. 11, 12). There is holy attire, too, which can glorify God (v. 9). This 'holy attire' (not the 'beauty of holiness' of older versions!) consists of the vestments which the priests of the

Lord put on when they led the temple worship. No detail in public worship or in private devotion is too small to demand our attention and obedience—'Majesty and splendour attend him, might and beauty are in his sanctuary' (v. 6).

The psalmist's God is both Creator (v. 5) and Judge (v. 13). This God is our God for ever.

LET US WORSHIP

He is the blessed and only Sovereign, King of kings and Lord of lords; he alone possesses immortality, dwelling in unapproachable light; him no one has ever seen or can ever see; to him be honour and dominion for ever! Amen.
(1 Timothy 6:15–16)

PSALM 97

A GREATER KING

This is another of the enthronement psalms—that is to say, psalms sung at the enthronement of a new king and on the anniversaries of that day (see the comment on Psalm 47 in *PBC Psalms 1—72* for more on enthronement psalms). They serve as useful occasions for their writers to point to another King, greater than any earthly one.

If we were to ask the writers of such psalms in what way or ways does Yahweh tower over the gods of the surrounding nations, they would probably reply: 'He is righteous; righteousness marks his uniqueness.' (Note verses 2 and 6; note also 'judgments' in verse 8). When a biblical writer says that his God is righteous, he does not mean merely that God does not do anything which is wrong. The word is much more positive and powerful than that. Because he has entered into a covenant with his people, he not only keeps true to that side of the relationship, but he takes dynamic action in implementing it. So 'righteousness' and 'salvation' are very closely connected. To take an example: in Judges 5:11, the words translated 'victories' and 'triumphs' are literally the 'righteousnesses' of the Lord. God is a God of action. He is Saviour and Rescuer.

It is, therefore, not surprising that the imagery used to describe Israel's God is powerful—cloud, fire, lightning-flashes; 'mountains melt like wax at the Lord's approach, the Lord of all the earth' (vv. 1–5). The puppet-gods of the surrounding nations make a poor showing when compared with the Lord. (See also Psalms 82:1 and 89:5–7.)

The followers of such a 'righteous' God should themselves be 'righteous' (v. 12), showing the marks of their Master, hating evil (v. 10), 'upright in heart' (v. 11) and joyful in the Lord (v. 12).

God's harvest

'A harvest of light' (v. 11)—the phrase is unusual. How can we illustrate its meaning? You are given a pot of bulbs. There is no sign of anything above the soil. You put it in a warm cupboard during the cold period. Then you bring it out into the light. That is what is needed. It will not be long before you have flowers in plenty. Or, here is a field, well ploughed and planted with seed. Your hopes of a good harvest are high. But this particular year, the clouds are leaden, week after week. Unless the clouds part and light shines on that field, your harvest will be a disaster. God has high hopes for his children, for their growth, their development, their flowering.

LET US PRAY

May the God of hope fill us with all joy and peace in believing.

MARVELLOUS DEEDS

Verse 1: there are several times within the Psalter when the various writers call upon us to 'sing a new song to the Lord'. May we take this as a gentle warning against staleness in worship? It is all too easy to succumb to the temptation of a thoughtless repetitiveness. Jesus himself must have had such thoughts in mind when he warned his friends not to 'go babbling on like the heathen' (Matthew 6:7).

What particular events had our psalmist in mind when he referred to God's 'marvellous deeds' and 'his right hand and holy arm' which 'have won him victory'? (v. 1; similar language is used in Isaiah 52:10). It may well be a reference to the Exodus when God rescued the Israelites from Pharaoh's cruel bondage. That is the supreme salvation-operation to which the biblical writers constantly looked back. Or perhaps the psalmist had in mind some more recent victory. Perhaps both; we cannot tell. What is clear is that he is expressing his belief in a God who intervenes in history and, through history, makes his character known. (See also Psalm 105.)

As a true poet, our writer enlists history, music, and nature to help him in his paean of praise to the Almighty. In verses 1–3, he calls on history, past events which must never be forgotten. In verses 4–6, he calls on music, vocal and instrumental. In verses 7–9, he calls on nature, the sea, the rivers, the mountains, 'to clap their hands' and 'sing aloud together before the Lord'. It is a majestic concept.

An eye to the future

But the psalmist's range of vision is not narrowed to the past nor even to the present. He has an eye to the future as well. The Lord comes to judge: 'He will judge the world with justice' (v. 9). History is moving to a climax, a consummation when earth's wrongs will be righted and, in Paul's phrase, 'God will be all in all' (1 Corinthians 15:28). Today, in Jewish worship, in the home ritual of Passover-time, a cup of wine is poured for the prophet Elijah who, it is believed, will return to herald 'the great and terrible day of the Lord' (Malachi 4:5). In Christian worship, every time the Eucharist is celebrated, it is 'until he come'. Exactly how or precisely when 'he will come in glory to judge the living and the dead', as the creed puts it, we do not know; the pages of history are strewn with examples of people who have tried to foretell the details, with disastrous results. But a theology which pays no heed to the coming consummation of all things in Christ is a poor, truncated thing. Jesus drew the picture of a time when the Son of Man would 'sit on his glorious throne, with all the nations gathered before him... he will place the sheep on his right hand and the goats on his left...' (Matthew 25:31ff.). Only the foolish will fail to heed this truth.

LET US PRAY

Almighty God,
give us grace to cast away the works of darkness
and to put on the armour of light,
now in the time of this mortal life,
in which your Son Jesus Christ came to us
in great humility:
so that on the last day,
when he shall come again in his glorious majesty
to judge the living and the dead,
we may rise to the life immortal;
through him who is alive and reigns
with you and the Holy Spirit,
one God, now and for ever.

Collect for Advent Sunday, *Alternative Service Book 1980*

HOLINESS

This is another enthronement psalm (see Psalms 47, 97, etc.). In commenting on Psalm 98, we noted the danger of repetitiveness in worship. Repetition, however, is a very different matter. To be 'repetitive' is to repeat something pointlessly, to no purpose. Repetition is to repeat something deliberately, with a clear and defined purpose. For instance, the repetition of a word or phrase in a poem or psalm can be a powerful means of fastening a concept in the mind. Psalm 99 illustrates this well. Three strong hammer-blows should ensure that the nail is in place. 'Holy is he,' says verse 3. 'Holy is he,' says verse 5. Then, with a slight elaboration of the refrain, 'Holy is the Lord our God,' says verse 9. The holiness of God is the main theme of this psalm.

When young Isaiah's hero-king (Uzziah) died in disgrace, the prophet had a vision of another King greater than any other earthly monarch. He heard the seraphim calling to one another, 'Holy, holy, holy is the Lord of Hosts: the whole earth is full of his glory' (Isaiah 6:3; seraphim are thought of as heavenly beings in attendance on God, as earthly rulers were attended by a courtly retinue).

Soliloquy and exhortation

The psalm hovers strangely between a kind of soliloquy with God and an exhortation to those for whom the psalmist is writing. In soliloquy with God, he uses such phrases as 'your great and terrible name' (v. 3), 'you have established equity...' (v. 4), 'you answered... forgave... called them to account' (v. 8); in exhortation to worshippers he calls us to 'exalt the Lord our God and bow down' (vv. 5 and 9). The writer finds encouragement in the justice of God (v. 4), and in the fact that God answers prayer (v. 8). He illustrates this last point by giving three instances from Israel's history of men who interceded with God and whose prayers were heard (vv. 6–8). He had in mind the moving story of Moses when the Israelites had sinned—'If you will forgive them, forgive; but if not, blot out my name... from your book' (Exodus 32:30–35). He had in mind Aaron, who under somewhat similar circumstances, made expiation for the people, 'standing between the dead and the living, and the plague was stopped' (Numbers

16:46–50). He had in mind Samuel who 'prayed aloud to the Lord on behalf of Israel, and the Lord answered his prayer' (1 Samuel 7:8–9). He turns from history to the God of history—'You answered them; you... forgave' (v. 8).

We need more women and men who will read the history of their people, and who will read their daily newspaper, thoughtfully and prayerfully, in a spirit of soliloquy with God, recognizing that history is, in a real sense, 'His story'—that he is indeed the God of history. Such people will engage with him in a spirit of faith, praying for mercy, praying for justice and equity, meditating on the holiness of God.

LET US PRAY

With his seraph train before him,
With his holy Church below,
Thus unite we to adore him,
Bid we thus our anthem flow:

'Lord, thy glory fills the heaven;
Earth is with its fullness stored;
Unto thee be glory given.
Holy, holy, holy, Lord.'

Bishop Richard Mant (1776–1848)

JUBILATE!

Let us do a bit of language study. It can be fun. It can also give us a clue to the meaning of a word or a passage in a book.

Psalm 100 is known to many people as the Jubilate. That is a Latin word, which simply means 'be joyful! Jubilate!' We recognize it in the word Jubilee. That, in turn, comes from a Hebrew word which means ram's horn. That instrument of music was blown when the Jews felt they must celebrate some outstanding feature of their history as, for example, their rescue from Egyptian tyranny. If you want an interesting read, turn to Leviticus. There you will read the directions to be carried out every fiftieth year: 'Hallow the fiftieth year and proclaim liberation in the land for all its inhabitants... The fiftieth year is to be a jubilee for you' (Leviticus 25:10, 11). The ram's horn was to be blown throughout the land to summon the people. The land was to rest. The people were to go to their homes. Freedom and joy were in the air! They could and they should jubilate!

Verse 3: in the Authorized Version and in the old Prayer Book, this verse ran, 'Know ye that the Lord he is God: and it is he that hath made us and not we ourselves; we are his people and the sheep of his pasture'. 'And not we ourselves' sounds a little strange. By the exchange of one Hebrew letter, and with no difference in sound, the words mean 'we are his'. This is stronger:

He made us
and we are his,
his own people,
the flock which he shepherds.

That is something to jubilate about! That is the reason that we can 'acclaim the Lord' (v. 1), 'enter his gates with thanksgiving... and bless his name' (v. 4).

A celebratory people

Who is the speaker who is calling on people to 'acclaim the Lord'? Probably we can envisage a priest as he welcomes pilgrims to the temple in Jerusalem and throws open the gates to admit them to the courts of the Lord (v. 4) for celebratory worship.

When the Franciscans were compiling a new version of the Daily Office (the regular daily services of the Church), they called the book *Celebrating Common Prayer*. In choosing the word 'celebrating' they were reminding us that every day's prayers are celebrations of the goodness of God. Of course, we celebrate the Holy Communion when we gather round the table of the Lord; but the Franciscans are telling us to enter his courts with praise daily, even if these courts can only be a kitchen or a bedroom or a study.

God's children are celebratory people, singing people, because they are resurrection people. Even when, as sometimes happens, their voices are choked with tears, yet, in celebrating the cross and resurrection of Jesus, they can steady themselves in his everlasting love (v. 5).

TO PONDER

'I am convinced that there is nothing in death or life... nothing in all creation that can separate us from the love of God in Christ Jesus our Lord' (Romans 8:38–39). This is the Christian's rock of confidence in a shifting world. Thanks be to God.

KEEPING WATCHFUL

A thoughtful reading of this psalm may well leave the reader with a feeling of unease. The first six verses all begin with 'I'. And it must be admitted that, in addition to its egocentricity, there is a note of superiority, of boasting, about the psalm. Isn't the writer a bit over-pious? Well, we hope that he was more concerned with his intention than with his description of himself! Sometimes, as we shall see in Psalm 119, it is not pride or false piety simply to be grateful for the gift of faith and the grace of obedience to God's will.

That having been said, it is a fact that the writer puts his finger with a sure touch on areas of life where a godly person needs to keep watchful. In the course of ordinary day-by-day living, there are many occasions where he can trip up, and the shine of his discipleship is dulled. For example:

The home (v. 2). The very intimacy of family relationships calls for extra watchfulness. Sometimes we are less courteous with our close relatives than we are with our business companions or social friends. We take for granted those under our own roof.

The eyes (v. 3a). Jesus had a sharp word to say about 'lustful eyes' (Matthew 5:27ff.). Apparently, sexual harassment is not a new phenomenon!

The thoughts (v. 4). What are crooked thoughts? We say of a good man, 'He's straight. We could trust him in a business deal, or when we buy a car off him, or when he is reporting a story. He's straight.'

The tongue (v. 5a). 'Of course, my dear, I wouldn't tell a soul but you. But did you know that she...' And so the scandal goes the rounds, and each time it goes, it grows. We would do well to read the letter of James regularly, and especially 3:1–12.

The companions (v. 6). This does not mean a priggish aloofness from those who do not share our faith. We have much to learn from them and we are privileged to have their friendship. But we need the company of Christians stronger than ourselves, of women and men with whom we regularly worship, and with whom we can speak freely of the things of God. This requires both a positive desire to 'choose the good' and, as we see in verses 7 and 8, an equally positive determination to reject the evil. There is a sentence in Malachi 3:16 which runs, 'Then those who feared the Lord talked together, and the Lord paid heed and listened.' And Jesus said, 'Where two or three meet together in my name, I am there among them' (Matthew 18:20). The presence of God is most readily found in the company of those who seek it.

PRAYER

Set a watch, O Lord, before our eyes,
our thoughts,
our tongues,
and grant that, in the company of your people,
we may grow strong in faith,
in hope,
in love.

PSALM 102

A Sick Man

The pendulum of this psalm swings wide—in terms of space, from the personal through the national, to the international; in terms of time, from man's brief life-span to God's eternity.

Space. The psalmist is deeply concerned about his personal situation. He is a sick man. He mentions his fever (v. 3), his loss of appetite (v. 4), his loss of weight (v. 5), his sleeplessness and sense of loneliness (v. 7), the antipathy of his enemies (v. 8), and, like a black cloud behind all his other ills, a sense of God's anger (vv. 10, 23). From his concern for his own person, he passes to the ills of his nation, his beloved Zion (vv. 13, 14) for whose restoration he longs (v. 16). From the national, his thoughts turn to the international (vv. 15, 22).

Time. He realizes the brevity of his life-span, the frailty of his frame (vv. 11, 23), indeed of the universe itself (vv. 25, 26). In a passage of great power, he contrasts this with the eternity of God (vv. 25ff.; the verses are quoted in Hebrews 1:10–12).

There are other psalms which cover much of the same ground (see, for example, Psalm 39), but they rarely display such force as does this Psalm 102. It has an enviable quality of frankness and honesty about it. The psalmist is prepared to tell God exactly how he feels, and from that position of dependence he is able to experience the faithfulness (v. 27) and the mercy (v. 13) of the Lord.

Guidelines for prayer

Most of those who read this book spend a few minutes each day in prayer, seek to keep to it regularly, and want to develop it. This often involves struggle for all of us, and the first to understand the difficulties, for example, of a mother with children or someone with long working hours is—God! This psalm offers us some helpful guidelines:

(i) It encourages us to spill out before God our griefs, fears, troubles, hopes. The saying 'a trouble shared is a trouble halved' is true, and if the trouble is shared with God, the relief is all the greater. Spill it out—and linger a moment in God's presence.

(ii) The psalmist suggests that we should keep the horizons of our prayers wide open. All too easily we narrow the boundaries of our prayers to the limit of our home or parish. There is a world out there which God loves. He bids us share his concern for it with him.

(iii) Our psalmist cared deeply for the sacred city of Zion. We scarcely need reminding that Jerusalem is a focal point of Middle East tension. Humanly speaking, there seems to be little prospect of finding a solution to the problem. 'Pray for the peace of Jerusalem...' (Psalm 122:6).

TO PONDER

Jesus told his disciples 'a parable to show that they should keep on praying and never lose heart' (Luke 18:1).

Lord, teach us how to pray aright,
With reverence and with fear;
though dust and ashes in thy sight
We may, we must, draw near.

J. Montgomery (1771–1854)

A HAPPY PSALM

This happy psalm obviously comes from the pen of a man with a full and grateful heart. It is a meditation on the character of God himself, as he deals with the psalmist as an *individual*, pardoning, healing (v. 3), rescuing, crowning (v. 4), satisfying and renewing him (v. 5). Then he ranges out over God's dealings with his *people* (v. 7), manifesting his father-like compassion. The human race is frail and short-lived; God's love and righteousness are unending (vv. 15ff.; there are parallels with Psalm 102:23–28). The language and the imagery are very powerful. God's love 'towers high' above the earth (v. 11). He has put our sins as far away from us 'as east is from west' (v. 12). Human life is as transitory as a wild flower in the meadow (vv. 15, 19).

Bless the Lord

In this and in many following psalms, we shall find the phrase 'bless the Lord'. It trips off the tongue easily, for we have become accustomed to it. But what did the psalmist mean by it? For that matter, what do we mean by it? It is natural for us to ask God to bless us—we in our poverty need his beneficence every moment. But God does not need to be told how great he is! Flattery is no part of worship.

Let us imagine two scenes:

(i) We are standing overlooking the Grand Canyon or the Victoria Falls—a natural phenomenon of extreme power and beauty. Probably our first reaction is one of awed silence—we are struck dumb. And that is right. But at last we cannot hold back—we fumble for words. Wonder, in the presence of nature, music, art, releases floods of praise. It is the natural outflowing in the presence of something wholly admirable. Wonder is next to worship. The *Benedicite* ('O all ye works of the Lord... O ye angels... O ye heavens...'), which perhaps used to bore us when we tried to sing it in church, is only an attempt to express the inexpressible. We shall see more of this when we come to Psalm 104.

(ii) Here is an engaged couple. They are head-over-heels in love. He finds himself telling her how wonderful she is. Should we dismiss this as mere sloppiness? I think not. To him it is irresistible—it must come out! And in the doing of this, he himself becomes a bigger man, less self-centred, more open to what is beautiful and true.

In the Eucharist, apart from the intercessions, the main emphasis of the service is one of praise and thanksgiving. Indeed, the word Eucharist means just that—thanksgiving. Thanksgiving, adoration, blessing, do something to push us out from the shallows of self-centredness into the ocean of God's love.

May we not believe that God receives with joy our splutterings when we 'bless' him? And in that act, whether it is in silence or in words, do we not become more after the pattern he has designed for us?

TO PONDER

Let us bless the Lord.
Thanks be to God.

The GIFT of LIFE

Enjoy this psalm! It is a great poem. Before you examine it in any detail, read it through at a run. If you own a video of one of David Attenborough's nature films, play it as a commentary on this psalm. And if you want a good read which fills out this psalm, you could try Ecclesiasticus 42:15—43:33 in the Apocrypha. This psalm is an invitation to us to stop and look:

> *What is this life if, full of care,*
> *We have no time to stand and stare?* (W. H. Davies)

I shall never forget the leisurely moments I spent in a car looking straight into the eyes of a lion in Africa, and the feeling of a certain oneness with him in the gift of the life that flowed through each of us.

Grand procession

Our poet ranges widely. Under his guidance, heaven and earth, winds and flames, seas and rivers, beasts and birds, grass and grain, wine and oil pass before us in grand procession. He is enjoying himself, and he is sure that God enjoys himself as creator and caretaker of it all (v. 31). A probable translation of verse 26 is: 'Sea-monsters swim therein, Leviathan which you formed for yourself as a plaything.' In this, the psalmist is at one with the writer of the first of the Genesis creation stories: after the record of God's creative acts comes the refrain 'and God saw that it was *good*'. (One can imagine a carpenter who has made a beautiful table standing back, rubbing his hands, and saying: 'That's *good*!')

If, as we are suggesting, it is right to think of God as enjoying his creation and delighting in it, should we not be hearing more about God's enjoyment of and delight in that particular part of it which is humankind? 'God created human beings in his own image... and God saw all that he had made, and it was very good' (Genesis 1:27, 31). Granted, that idyllic picture is of humankind before the 'Fall'. But God does not love us because we are good. He loves us for what we are and for what we can become. The father's arms were around the returning prodigal son not because he was good—he doubtless still smelt of the pig sty!—but because he was a son of his father's begetting, with the promise of a future of limitless possibilities. Julian of Norwich wrote, 'He loves us and enjoys us, and he wills that we love him and enjoy him, and firmly trust him; and all shall be well.' And again, 'He delights in us for ever, as we shall in him, by his grace.'

The implications of this emphasis on God's attitude to his creation are clear: the physical world is sacred and must be treated with reverence. It was a West African who wrote:

> *Enjoy the world gently,*
> *Enjoy the world gently,*
> *For if the earth is spoiled*
> *It cannot be repaired.*
> *Enjoy the world gently.*

What is true of the physical world is true of human beings. However depraved they are, they are to be loved as children of the Most High.

TO PONDER

He who has ears to hear, let him hear.
He who has eyes to see, let him use them,
and using them, let him adore.

PSALM 105

PACKED VERSES

How much the psalmist packs into the opening six verses of this psalm! He touches on worship: 'give thanks' (v. 1a), 'pay him honour...' (v. 2a), 'exult...' (v. 3a). He touches on what we might call evangelism: 'make known...' (v. 1b), 'tell...' (v. 2b). He touches on the secret of spiritual strength: 'look to the Lord... seek his presence' (v. 4), 'remember the marvels he has wrought...' (v. 6). That is guidance for godliness—in a nutshell!

If the main accent in Psalm 104 was on God's activity in nature, the main accent in this psalm is on his activity in history. The writer sees God as the One who entered into an agreement with his people, a covenant to which he ever remains faithful. Abraham, Isaac and Jacob are the central figures (vv. 9 and 10) and the seminal passage is Genesis 12:1–9, where we see Abraham daringly striding out of the security of his household into the unknown. He went, as Hebrews 11:8–10 puts it, 'without knowing where he was to go', yet obeying the call 'by faith'.

Retelling the story

The rest of the psalm is a résumé of the story of the wilderness wanderings, the great famine and the part played by Joseph in making provision for the famished people (vv. 17–22; see Genesis 39ff.), the arrival of Israel in Egypt (vv. 23–25; see Exodus 1:6–22), the appearance of Moses and Aaron (vv. 26–27; see Exodus 2), the plagues (vv. 28–36; see Exodus 7ff.), and the rescue of the Israelites in the great drama of the Exodus (vv. 37–42; see Exodus 12:37ff.).

'A small company it was, few in number, strangers... roaming' (vv. 12, 13). And a strange figure at the heart of the whole Exodus episode—Moses! A murderer (see Exodus 2:11–15), a hesitant man —'Lord, send anyone else you like' (Exodus 4:13). It would seem that God does not depend on numbers nor on dynamic leaders for the achievement of his purposes. The achievement of the Exodus, to which future generations were to look back as the signal example of God's rescuing activity, came about not because of human power and expertise, but in spite of human paucity in numbers and perversity in response to the divine will.

As Paul went on his journeys, founding and strengthening little groups of new disciples, they must have seemed to him to be pathetically weak, but he was not dismayed. God, he wrote, 'has chosen things without rank or standing in the world, mere nothings, to overthrow the existing order'. Why? 'So no place is left for any human pride in the presence of God. By God's act you are in Christ Jesus' (1 Corinthians 1:28–30).

TO PONDER

'Little is much when God is in it.' Think of instances in recent history, or in your own experience, where this is true.
'A small company it was...'
'Lord, send anyone else you like... I am slow and hesitant...'
Then—take heart! God might enlist you.

FAITHLESS PEOPLE

This writer cared deeply for the nation of which he was a member, and longed for its spiritual welfare. Like the writer of Psalm 105, he looked back over its history. But whereas the writer of that psalm stresses the faithfulness of the God who had entered into a covenant-relationship with his people, the writer of this psalm stresses the faithlessness of a people who, time and time again, failed to live up to their part of the agreement.

The verbs he uses sound like a death-knell—'we have sinned, we have gone astray' (v. 6), 'they soon forgot' (vv. 13, 21), 'they tried God's patience' (v. 14), 'they made a calf' (v. 19), 'they rejected... they muttered treason' (vv. 24, 25), and so on. Incidents from their history are chosen to illustrate the sorry story: for example, the making of a lifeless idol (v. 28), the grumbling at Meribah, 'the place of strife' (v. 32; see Numbers 20:13). The leaders Moses (v. 23) and Phinehas (v. 30) are singled out as intervening, interceding, on behalf of the people and their injured God. The language used to describe the offence caused to God by the people's sin—his purpose to destroy the people (v. 23), to strike them down (v. 26), his anger (vv. 29, 32, 40), his loathing of them (v. 40), and so on—distresses us even though it is softened by references to his pity (v. 44), his boundless love (v. 45), his compassion (v. 46). The psalmist is trying to find language to convey God's detestation of national sin, the breach of covenant by which a nation turns from godliness to paganism, and the inexorable consequences of such conduct—dispersion among the nations (v. 27), plague (v. 29), defeat (vv. 41, 42). Before we jettison such a picture of an angry God, should we not give some thought to what indeed happens when holiness comes into collision with human sin and folly?

Dis-ease

It does not take a great deal of imagination to see the modern counterpart of what is described in verse 15. In the affluent West particularly, there is a society 'given what they asked'. Its members have voted for money in abundance, for a salacious press, for corrupt leadership, for noise, for dissipation—and they have got it in full measure. But is it meeting their deepest needs? By no means. It has been followed by 'a wasting sickness', a dis-ease at their vitals. We are breeding a race unable to think, fed on misleading soundbites, unable to endure silence, restless and not content to stand and stare, unable to ponder, still less to pray. A wasting disease is on the rampage. Forsaking the true God, we have fashioned for ourselves a pantheon of false gods. One by one they will topple and fall, and leave us stripped and naked. Then, and perhaps *only* then, God will, in his 'boundless love', 'relent' and rouse compassion for them in the hearts of their captors. He will 'call to mind his covenant' and deliver his people.

PRAYER

Deliver us, Lord our God... that we may give thanks to your holy name and make your praise our pride (v. 47).

The SOUND of PRAISE

At Psalm 107 we begin the last of the five books into which the Psalter is divided (see Introduction p. 19). The book contains within it fifteen psalms called 'Songs of the ascents' or 'pilgrim songs' (Psalms 120—134), and eight psalms prefaced, rather mysteriously, with the words 'for David' (Psalms 138—145). Were these psalms dedicated perhaps, to the 'Good King'? Or written for some royal event? The book also includes the longest of all the psalms, Psalm 119 (176 verses).

If we are to get the feel of these psalms and of Psalm 107 in particular, we should do well to note the sound of praise which runs through many of them. The centre of the life and worship of the people of Israel had been in Babylon, to which they had been deported. Something of what that meant to them is reflected in the wistful and bitter Psalm 137—'By the rivers of Babylon we sat down and wept as we remembered Zion... How could we sing the Lord's song in a foreign land?' (137:1 and 4). Now—as so many of these psalms indicate—God's people are back home, engaged in worship at God's temple in Jerusalem.

Ponder the Lord's deeds

Psalm 107 is a carefully crafted poem. We note its recurring refrain: 'Let them give thanks to the Lord for his love and for the marvellous things he has done for mankind' (vv. 8, 15, 21, 31). There is a genuine note about the psalmist's summons to the people to join him in his praises: 'It is good to give thanks to the Lord'. I can hear them shout back: 'For his love endures for ever' (v. 1).

The four main stanzas, beginning at verses 4, 10, 17 and 23, are Jewish history seen through the eyes of a deeply spiritual man. It would be easy to find passages in the Old Testament which would illustrate what he had in mind. But the writer is convinced that God is interested not only in past history. Up to verse 32 the verbs are in the past tense. At verse 33 they change into the present. God is not dead. He is active, both in judgment, turning rivers into desert (vv. 33–34), and in mercy (vv. 35ff.), rescuing, lifting the poor man clear, and so on. The psalm ends with an exhortation to 'lay these things to heart, and ponder the loving deeds of the Lord' in history and in present experience (v. 43).

There is much in this psalm which corresponds with the life experience of those who are seeking to live their lives under the Lordship of Christ. Perhaps as the result of an early conversion experience, they had thought that they were in for an easy run. Then they 'lost their way in desert wastelands'; 'their spirit', buoyed up by early hopes, 'was faint' until God 'rescued them' (stanza 1). Some 'sat in the dark', prisoners to their own depression or despair, till God 'brought them out of the dark... and burst their chains' (stanza 2). Some, well, it was their stupidity! As they looked back, they could see that they had only themselves to blame for getting into serious trouble. Then 'he saved them... he sent his word to heal them' (stanza 3). Others had experiences which were best described in terms of shipwreck (how the Jews hated the sea!) until, in God's mercy, 'the storm sank to a murmur' (stanza 4). It reminds us of the terrified disciples in the boat, terrified till they heard the Master's words: 'Silence! Be still!' (Mark 4:39).

PRAYER

Give me the wisdom to lay these things to heart and to ponder the loving deeds of the Lord.

PSALM 108

Verses 1–5 are virtually a repeat of Psalm 57:7–11, and verses 6–13 are virtually a repeat of Psalm 60:6–12. (See PBC *Psalms 1—72* for commentary.) Our 'book of Psalms' is, in fact, a small library of hymn books, and not surprisingly, some particularly popular 'hymns' are incorporated, in whole or in part, more than once in different sections of the book.

DEEP DISTRESS

This psalm is the cry of a deeply troubled man. If we want to find out what it is that is troubling him, the best way to do so is to read verses 1–7 and 21–25 together, before dealing with the rest of the psalm. The cause of his distress is twofold:

(i) He has been 'assailed' (v. 3) by a group of people and by one person in particular (v. 7, 'that rogue') who have maligned him, repaying evil for good, blackening his character.

(ii) He is sick, he cannot face food and is losing weight (vv. 23–24). His physical deterioration gives one more reason for his foes to mock him (v. 25). It is all the more difficult to stand up against blackmail when one's body is giving great trouble. So he cries out to God for help.

We must remember that our psalmist wrote long before the events of Christ's ministry and sacrifice on Calvary. He knew nothing of the One who 'when he was abused... did not retaliate, when he suffered... uttered no threats' (1 Peter 2:23). It is difficult enough for us who are on the right side of the Christ-event to follow the example of Jesus when we are the victims of unjust attack—how much more for the psalmist! We bear this in mind when we read verses 8–20, surely the bitterest tirade in the Psalter (see vv. 28 and 29). It is noteworthy that the writer calls down vengeance on one man in particular, presumably 'that rogue' of verse 7. We must remember, of course, that there were no 'quotation marks' in Hebrew texts, so it is sometimes hard to know who is 'speaking'. Some translations suggest that verses 8–14 are spoken by the psalmist's enemies.

Please read the pages on 'Imprecatory psalms' in the Introduction (pp. 21–23). For the psalmist, 'vengeance is mine, says the Lord' was every bit as much a foundational truth as the mercy of God. Justice was indivisible from holiness. Since writing those words, I have had the privilege of listening to a lecture by Michael Perham, Provost of Derby, from which I quote words which may help us when we read such passages as verses 8–20:

> *We... need to pray through the words of others... because sometimes it is*
> *these words that will enable us to pray to God about the emotions that we*

*are reluctant to feel or articulate... If you pray with the psalms, in a sense
you are given the freedom to pray to God the things that don't sound like
polite and proper prayers. The prayers that enable you to be angry with God;
the prayers that allow you to be depressed; the prayers that allow you to feel
that you are going under. We are all so well trained that we are not sure
that we ought to say that kind of thing to the Almighty, even when we are
feeling it... (God should only hear words of faith and trust!) Now the
psalms open up to us a world of people pouring out their hearts to God and
saying, in a sense, unacceptable things. For some of us that could be the
way in to being absolutely honest with God in prayer, and it is only then...
that we begin to receive from him the help we need.*

The sun comes out at verses 30 and 31. Faith triumphs over doubt,
hope over despair. The psalmist is assured of the justice of his God
in whom he has struggled to believe. The future is bright with the
confidence that once again he will extol God in the midst of his
worshipping people.

PRAYER

*Thou knowest, Lord, the secrets of our hearts; shut not thy merciful
ears to our prayer; but spare us, Lord most holy...*

PSALM 110

PRIEST & KING

This psalm, like Psalm 2 with which it has much in common, was probably used at the coronation ceremonies of a new king (see also Psalms 72, 101, 132). He is the 'my lord' of verse 1. God is represented as installing him at his right hand, that is the place of authority and power (vv. 5 and 6). He has the dew of youth still on him (v. 3), and he knows where to find resources of renewal for his task (v. 7).

This king is also a priest, 'a Melchizedek' in God's service. This takes us to Genesis 14:18–20 where we meet this mysterious figure—'King of Salem... priest of God Most High', who blessed Abram and gave him gifts. The only other place in Scripture where Melchizedek appears again is in the letter to the Hebrews. The writer makes the point that Christ and Melchizedek have this in common: they did not seek their position. They both were royal agents (Hebrews 5:1–6). In Hebrews 6:20—7:28, the writer describes Jesus as a high priest greater by far than Melchizedek, 'able to save completely those who approach God through him... suited to our need... made perfect for ever' (7:25, 26, 28).

Who precisely the psalmist had in mind when he wrote his description of God's appointee, it is difficult to say. The guesses of the commentators are many. Was it the newly anointed king? Was it a messianic figure? Was it the whole of Israel, 'a kingdom of priests'? However, one remark is relevant: as the Jews of our Lord's day read this description of their king 'crushing kings on the day of his wrath... shattering heads throughout the wide earth' (vv. 5 and 6), it is no wonder that they envisaged a coming Messiah who would drive the hated Roman occupiers off their land into the sea. With this in their minds, it was hard to conceive of a king entering Jerusalem 'in gentleness, riding on a donkey' (Matthew 21:5), a suffering Messiah who 'when he was abused... uttered no threats' (1 Peter 2:23). A people who had suffered much at the hands of their enemies found the way of forgiveness and peace extremely difficult. So, in their shoes, would we. Yet this (we must learn) is how God's power is 'made perfect in weakness'. As Paul was to put it, 'The folly of God is wiser than human wisdom, and the weakness of God stronger than human strength' (1 Corinthians 1:25).

TO PONDER AND TO PRAY

The Church is appointed by God to carry on the works of the Messiah, each member of the Church being a limb of Christ. Strengthened by the Holy Spirit, it fulfils its task in gentleness and humility.

Let us pray for the Church worldwide and for that part of it to which we belong:

Most gracious Father,
we pray for your holy catholic Church:
fill it with all truth
and in all truth with all peace;
where it is corrupt, purge it;
where it is in error, direct it;
where anything is amiss, reform it;
where it is right, strengthen and confirm it
where it is in want, furnish it;
where it is divided, heal it
and unite it in your love;
through Jesus Christ our Lord. Amen.

Celebrating Common Prayer, p. 249.

A THANKFUL HEART

This psalm, the first of a little group which begins, 'Praise the Lord', introduces us to a man with a thankful heart. Was he the leader of 'the congregation... the assembly' or simply one of the members of the group? It does not say. But the reason for his thankfulness is clear—it is God himself.

He elaborates the theme. He sees God's greatness in his activity—his works (v. 2), his deeds (vv. 3, 4)—and in his character—he is gracious and compassionate (v. 4), he provides for those who fear him, and he always keeps his covenant in mind (v. 5). Verses 6–9 underline what he has written in verses 2–5. He sums it all up in a sentence (v. 9b) which reminds us of the refrain in Psalm 99:1, 3, 9: 'Holy and awe-inspiring is his name' (his essential being, his character).

Special words

Two words call for our attention. They occur in the last verse of the psalm and they recur frequently in other parts of the Old Testament. They are 'fear' and 'beginning'.

(i) **Fear (vv. 5 and 10).** There are many instances when this word conveys the meaning which we usually attach to it in our literature and conversation: terror, dread, fright. But the word takes on the colour of its context and frequently has no suggestion of terror in it. It means reverence, profound respect, attention to the person concerned. It is in this sense that the word is used in verses 5 and 10.

(ii) **Beginning (v. 10).** Again, the word is used as we commonly use it, to convey the idea of a start to a life or project. Conceivably that might be its meaning in verse 10: a child's life begun in an atmosphere of reverence for God will continue to grow in understanding later on. We should note Proverbs 9:10, 11: the 'first step' to 'wisdom' is 'the fear of the Lord'.

But 'beginning' can also mean the chief or principal part, and it is likely that that is its meaning in verse 10: 'The fear of the Lord is the beginning of wisdom, and they who live by it grow in understanding.' The psalmist is not speaking about knowledge but about wisdom, and there is a great difference between the two. Knowledge has to do with 'knowing', with information and facts. Wisdom has to do with insight and understanding. Given a man or woman who has a deep reverence for God and is attentive to every indication of his will, there we may expect growth and understanding and the development of a healthy spiritual life. And the praise will be God's for ever (v. 10b).

PRAYER

Let us 'grow in grace and in the knowledge of our Lord and Saviour Jesus Christ' (2 Peter 3:18).

RELIGION *as* RELEASE

Here is a portrait of a good man. And of a happy one (v. 1)! True religion does not make people sour or gloomy or carping. It releases them from their fears and inhibitions. The one who 'fears the Lord' (v. 1; see Psalm 111 on the meaning of 'fear') finds deep delight in obedience to his commandments. It is significant that when Jesus was sketching the basic elements to be found in his followers, he began each one with the word 'blessed'. It is probable that in the language which he spoke, the word means 'oh the happinesses of...' (Matthew 5:3–12). Incidentally, that teaching can be seen as a corrective to the impression given by this psalm that, just because a person is godly, it follows that he will be prosperous! Jesus had some straight things to say about the dangers of wealth, of setting our hearts on riches, of the stranglehold which they can have on us (Matthew 6:19–21). Paul, in a chapter which gives us strong guidance on money and how to use it (2 Corinthians 9), warns us: 'Remember: sow sparingly and you will reap sparingly' (v. 6).

However, our psalmist sees that one of the marks of a person who fears the Lord is that he is 'gracious in his lending' (v. 5) and lavish in his gifts to the needy (v. 9). There is an interesting elaboration of this in the book of Tobit, written in the early part of the second century BC: 'All who give alms are making an offering acceptable to the Most High' (Tobit 4:7–11). The rich, in other words, must not cling to their wealth but share it, if they wish to please God.

Comfort for the anxious

'News of misfortune will have no terrors for him, because his heart is steadfast, trusting in the Lord' (v. 7). It was Peter, many years later, who wrote with all the wealth of his experience in the company of Christ: 'He cares for you, so cast all your anxiety on him' (1 Peter 5:7). It might almost be a comment on the psalmist's wise words. Here is comfort for the anxious, for those who pass long hours of foreboding in the night—what does the future hold for us, for our loved ones, for our church? 'He cares for you', you need not be anxious for the morrow. And one greater than Peter taught his friends to set their 'troubled hearts at rest. Trust in God always; trust also in me' (John 14:1).

The psalmist saw the person who fears the Lord as 'a beacon in darkness' (v. 4). Jesus saw his disciples as 'light for all the world' (Matthew 5:14).

PRAYER

Let us pray for a heart at rest, to soothe and sympathize with the anxious. Let us pray for grace to be 'a beacon in darkness', 'a light for all the world'.

PSALM 113

TRANSCENDENCE & IMMANENCE

Learned people who delight in long words would say that this psalm in its description of God stresses his transcendence and his immanence. By transcendence they mean his existence beyond the created world, his distance, his 'otherness'. By immanence they mean his presence in the world, his nearness to his creatures. Transcendence—'high is the Lord above all nations, high is his glory above the heavens... the Lord our God... who sets his throne so high' (vv. 4, 6). Immanence—he 'deigns to look down so low' (v. 6) and is concerned with the weak, the poor, the childless woman (vv. 7–9).

This psalm gives us an interesting glance into a society whose members are not buttressed by the help of any social services provided by the State. Our television screens show us the plight of the poverty-stricken, raking over the garbage heaps for scraps of food or for tins to sell. It all seems so far from the Western nations with their system of pensions, their departments of health and education; and so on. Our psalmist would imply that God is deeply concerned with the victims of such inequality. He would have no truck with the stanza in the hymn 'All things bright and beautiful' which, in earlier hymn books, ran:

The rich man in his castle
The poor man at his gate
He made them high and lowly
And ordered their estate.

To understand the last verse of our psalm, we need to remember that in biblical times the lot of a childless couple was blamed solely on the woman; she was even thought to be under God's frown. People knew nothing of male infertility. The moving story of the childless Hannah, tormented by her rival-wife Peninnah, but eventually conceiving and bearing a son, Samuel, is told in 1 Samuel 1 and is well worth reading.

Caring for 'little ones'

Matthew tells the story of the disciples' debate about 'who is the greatest'. Jesus took a child for his object lesson. Three times over in this passage he spoke about the little ones, and then about the one lost sheep (Matthew 18:1–14). God, so he would say, takes no notice of status. He is concerned about people and their needs. God 'raises the poor from the rubbish heap' (v. 7), and calls us to share in this compassionate ministry.

PRAYER

O God our king, exalted on high,
yet stooping to the measure of our lowliness,
you have called us to be holy for you are holy:
as in our worship we confess your glory,
so may our lives be directed in righteousness;
through Jesus Christ our Lord.

Celebrating Common Prayer, p. 614

PSALM 114

STORY *of* DEPARTURE

Exodus 14 is essential reading if we are to appreciate this poem. 'Exodus' simply means departure, and Exodus 14 is the story of the departure of all departures, the escape of the Israelites from the tyranny of Egypt. Year after year, around countless camp-fires, the story was told and, no doubt, as is the way of stories re-told, was added to.

Here the psalmist could assume that his readers knew the story well. He added the poet's touch. He was not afraid to write of fleeing seas and skipping hills (vv. 3, 4)—that is a way that poets have! He addresses the sea; he addresses the Jordan: 'What made you do that?' They give no reply, but the poet knows: it was 'the presence of the Lord, the presence of the God of Jacob' (v. 7). For good measure, in the closing verse, he refers to another instance in their history, when God acted in power on behalf of his people and water flowed from the rock—'the flinty cliff' became 'a welling spring' (see Numbers 20:6–13).

God's purpose

Verses 1 and 2: God had a purpose in mind when he rescued Israel from 'a barbaric people' and settled them in their own land. It was that Judah should become 'God's sanctuary, Israel his domain'. To be a worshipping community, a kingdom of holiness, was the destiny of the Jewish people. Down the centuries, people have questioned God's 'choice' of this particular people. How odd (they say) that he should give one race this specific destiny. But the writer of Psalm 114 did not think it odd. In the midst of nations worshipping many gods there was to be a sanctuary where the one true God would be worshipped, one nation faithful to the God who called it (see Psalm 147:19, 20).

It is impossible to over-emphasize the importance of the Exodus in the Old Testament and in later Jewish thought. God 'made bare his holy arm' (rolled up his sleeves, as we would say); 'his right hand, his holy arm have won him victory' (Psalm 98:1). In Christian thinking, we regard the Exodus as a kind of foreshadowing of the delivery achieved by the saving activity of Jesus in his dying and in his resurrection. When Luke tells the story of Jesus' transfiguration, he says that Moses and Elijah, who talked with him on the mountain, spoke of his departure, 'his exodus which he was about to fulfil in Jerusalem' (Luke 9:31). His choice of the word 'exodus' may have hinted at the significance of the saving work of God's Son in rescuing his people from a tyranny worse and more universal than the tyranny of the Jews under Egyptian rule—the tyranny of sin and death. It was a divine achievement and a 'full-filment' of the Old Testament story, a divine act of saving power. And the God who delivered long ago still delivers his people (see 2 Corinthians 1:10–11).

PRAISE

God set us free to worship without fear, holy and righteous
all the days of our life.

GLORYING *in* GOD'S GRACE

The psalmist is amazed at the grace of God, his sheer love and faithfulness (v. 1). He glories in it. This is a major theme in the New Testament. Paul especially makes much of God's grace. He wrote to the Galatians: 'God forbid that I should boast of anything but the cross of our Lord Jesus Christ' (Galatians 6:14); and to the Romans: 'What room… is left for human pride? It is excluded' (Romans 3:27). We come with empty hands to God, for only he can cleanse us, set us on our feet.

The biting satire of verses 4–8 is repeated in Psalm 135:15–18 and reaches its climax in the stinging words: 'Their makers become like them', that is, senseless and useless (Psalm 115:8 and 135:18). There are similar passages in the prophetical books, for example Isaiah 41:21–24, 29 and 44:9–20. The idols are ineffective and ridiculous. In contrast, Israel's God is 'a help and a shield' (vv. 9, 10, 11).

Verses 9–11, with that threefold refrain, 'He is their help and their shield', sound like a piece of liturgy—the priest saying the first line and the congregation responding with the refrain. The remaining verses of the psalm could also have been used liturgically. The threefold division 'Israel', 'the house of Aaron', 'those who fear the Lord' (vv. 9–11, and repeated in vv. 12–13) is interesting. The writer thinks first of his nation, Israel; he proceeds to the priestly tribe of Aaron; he ends with 'those who fear the Lord'. This last phrase obviously includes the first two classes but it reaches out to include Gentiles who were drawn to the religion of Israel and to Israel's God. Of these there were many, people who saw through the emptiness of polytheism and were attracted to the ethics (if not to the sacrifices) of the Jewish faith. (See also Psalm 118:1 and Psalm 135:19, 20.)

Blessing

The congregation having played its part (vv. 9–13), the priest then gives the blessing (vv. 14–15). Or perhaps the blessing ends at verse 16, and the people respond with verses 17 and 18 (note 'we, the living…' in verse 18).

'The dead… those who go down to the silent grave' (v. 17): we have encountered the idea of Sheol, the place of silence, of shades and shadows, in previous psalms. Here it is again. There is no praising God in Sheol—so, while we have breath, we will praise him. The psalmists wrote on the wrong side of Christ's resurrection, if we may put it that way. That epoch-making event has transfigured our idea of death and what is after it. 'After that,' the writer of Revelation says, 'I looked and saw a vast throng… and they shouted aloud: "Victory to our God who sits on the throne, and to the Lamb!"' (Revelation 7:9, 10). And again: 'After this I heard what sounded like a vast throng in heaven shouting: "Hallelujah! Victory and glory and power belong to our God"' (Revelation 19:1). How much more cause for joyful praise and thanksgiving have we than the psalmist long ago!

PRAISE

Let us join in this shout!

The GREAT 'I AM'

This splendid psalm is a personal tribute to the goodness of God. The writer wants whomever will listen to know of God's graciousness and compassion as he himself has experienced it. Clearly, he had come near to death (v. 3), he had been brought low (v. 6), reduced to tears (v. 8), in bitter distress (v. 10), disillusioned by the faithlessness of his friends (v. 11). And all the time the sinister prospect of Sheol like a chill fog oppressed him (v. 3; see Psalm 115).

The dead 'cannot praise the Lord' (Psalm 115:17); it is the task of the living, of those who have experienced his grace. God had answered his cry for help. He bears his witness to that in language which is simple and sincere. No wonder that he loved his God and delighted to invoke him 'by name' (vv. 4 and 13)—an unusual phrase. Presumably he means the name of Yahweh, the great 'I am', or 'I will be' (see Exodus 3:14). This God of Abraham, Isaac and Jacob, who had seen them through their crises, could be relied upon to see him through his trouble.

In verses 7 and 8 he engages in a little soliloquy. He addresses himself: 'My heart, be at peace once more.' He addresses God: 'You have rescued me.' It is a good way to pray. Sometimes, especially in times of great distress, all we can manage, and all that is needed, is the two words 'my God', or 'oh God'. These words, so often used thoughtlessly, can be a means of communication between us and God; God can be trusted to fill in what is in our hearts and cannot be expressed through our lips.

Dedicated to God

The psalmist asks himself how he can repay such a lavish and prayer-answering God (v. 12). He answers as any religious Jew would do, by saying he will pay his vows, his animal offerings as laid down in the law. The cup of salvation (v. 13) may be a reference to the drink-offering mentioned in Exodus 29:40. He will be present with all God's people in God's house in Jerusalem (vv. 14, 18, 19). If his loyalty to God were to involve him even in death, that offering would be precious to God (v. 15). As it is, he offers himself to God as his willing slave, for God is the one who had loosed his bonds (v. 16). His determination to live a life dedicated to God is expressed by the repetition of 'I shall' (vv. 9, 13, 14, 17, 18).

In commending our faith to a friend or colleague, more powerful than any sermon or book is the witness of a life lived consistently as God's slave. The next most powerful witness is that of our lips, in a few words of sincere testimony—'Let me tell you what God has done for me' or '...what Christ means to me', or '...the difference that being a disciple of Jesus means to me' or '...the strength that comes to me through worshipping with God's people in God's house'; or, in the words of verse 1: 'I love the Lord, for he has heard me and listened to my prayer.' The psalmist has much to teach us.

TO PONDER

The God who looses our bonds can also loose our tongues.

SHORT *but* EXUBERANT

This, the shortest psalm in the Psalter, is also the last of the 'Praise the Lord' group which began at Psalm 111.

There is an exuberance about it—all nations, all peoples are summoned to praise Yahweh, not their old gods whom our writer (or a fellow psalmist) had mocked in Psalm 115. The author of Psalm 148 casts his net even wider: he calls not only on nations and peoples but also on angels, sun and moon, animals, elements, cattle and birds, kings and commoners, boys and girls to join in the chorus of praise.

The writer of Psalm 117 has a theological basis for the summons to praise which he issues. It is twofold: God's protecting love, and his everlasting faithfulness. If we were to ask the psalmist, 'What is God faithful to?' he would probably answer, 'To the covenant he has made.' And if we were to ask further, 'What covenant?' he might well refer us to the story in Genesis about Noah and the flood, and God's promise never again to put the earth under a curse. 'As long as the earth lasts, seedtime and harvest, cold and heat, summer and winter, day and night, they will never cease' (Genesis 8:21, 22). God then gives Noah a sign: 'This is the sign which I am giving of the covenant between myself and you and all living creatures with you: my bow I set in the clouds to be a sign of the covenant between myself and the earth' (Genesis 9:12, 13).

Love and faithfulness

For a Christian, these two words 'love' and 'faithfulness' have a far deeper content than they could have had for the psalmist. 'This is how God showed his love among us,' writes John: 'he sent his only Son into the world that we might have life through him' (1 John 4:9). And as for God's faithfulness to his covenant-relationship with his people, we are reminded of a new covenant every time we take part in a Eucharist service. 'Drink this,' we hear the celebrant say, 'all of you; this is my blood of the new covenant, which is shed for you and for many for the forgiveness of sins.'

We should not under-estimate the value of this psalm just because it is short. When we are depressed and tempted to think that 'the struggle nought availeth, the labour and the wounds are vain' (Arthur

Hugh Clough), we can recall days when God has kept our feet from falling and we have shared in the strong love which has protected us, and the everlasting faithfulness which is an aspect of God's grace. This is, of course, a constant theme of the psalms. The Lord is 'my refuge and fortress' (Psalm 91:2).

Have the psalmist and George Herbert, the poet, met in heaven? I like to think of the psalmist teaching the poet his little psalm, and the poet teaching the psalmist his hymn:

Seven whole days, not one in seven
I will praise thee;
In my heart, though not in heaven,
I can raise thee.
Small it is, in this poor sort
to enrol thee:
E'en eternity's too short
to extol thee.

LET US PRAISE
We will join the psalmist and the poet.
'We will trust and not be afraid.'

PSALM 118 ✓

To the TEMPLE

This lively and interesting psalm takes us to the temple at Jerusalem.
We seek to join the people in their worship on a particularly joyful
day: 'This is the day on which the Lord has acted, a day for us to exult
and rejoice' (v. 24), a day for celebration. It opens with a summons
to worship (vv. 1–4). (For the three groups summoned, see Psalm
115:9–11.) The people have a leader, presumably their king; much of
the psalm is personal—'I called to the Lord' (v. 5), 'I drove them off'
(v. 12), 'I shall not die' (v. 17) and so on. In the presence of his
people, the leader bears his witness to the goodness of God. (On the
power of such a testimony, see the comment on Psalm 116.)

A major victory

Clearly, there has been a major national victory over menacing
nations who swarmed round the people and their king like bees (v.
12). It was a chastening experience, but God had won the day—we
note the threefold emphasis on God's right hand (vv. 15 and 16).
Now it is only right and proper that there should be a great service
of thanksgiving, just as there was in London when the people, led
by Winston Churchill himself, met in St Margaret's Church, West-
minster, at the end of World War II. People and king swarm up to the
temple gates. 'Open to me the gates of victory,' says their leader on
behalf of them all, and the gate-keepers answer with a welcome (vv.
19, 20). 'I shall praise you, for you have answered me,' says the king,
for God's deliverance 'is wonderful in our eyes' (vv. 19–23). It is a day
never to be forgotten… 'a day for us to exult and rejoice' (v. 24).

The welcome from the temple authorities is cordial: 'Blessed is he
who enters in the name of the Lord; we bless you from the house of
the Lord' (v. 26). Indeed they invite the worshippers to engage in a
festal dance right up to the altar itself (v. 27)—the 'cords' may have
been festal branches which the people had brought with them; as
they touched each other, the unity of the worshippers was enhanced.
'You are my God and I shall praise you,' says the king; and the people
shout back with the words with which the psalm began: 'It is good
to give thanks to the Lord, for his love endures for ever' (v. 29).

This psalm could well have been set to music, with different voices

112

taking the part of king and of priest, and the whole choir taking the chorus. The constant use of repetition lends itself to antiphonal singing. For example, part of the choir would sing verse 6, the other part verse 7; part of the choir would sing verse 8, the other part verse 9. Other examples of such antiphonal singing suggest themselves in this psalm.

The verses in this psalm most familiar to readers are verses 22 and 23 because they are quoted or referred to in the New Testament (by Jesus in Matthew 21:42, by Peter in Acts 4:11, and in 1 Peter 2:6). The cornerstone held the building together and gave it stability; it must be large and strong. It was God's purpose that Israel should be that cornerstone in the building of his kingdom. The nations of the world did not see it that way. They rejected it. But—here the psalmist shares God's vision and in faith sees the operation as already completed—that stone, rejected by men, has been the top-stone which gloriously completes the building.

In the Christian scheme of things, Christ as the centre of the new Israel was indeed despised and rejected of men, but raised by God to the place of honour above all others. That was the Lord's doing and it is marvellous in our eyes.

LET US BE GLAD

Christ is our Cornerstone,
On him alone we build;
With his true saints alone
The courts of heaven are filled:
On his great love
Our hopes we place
Of present grace
And joys above.

Trs. J. Chandler (1806–76)

113

PRAYER & DIALOGUE

A casual reading of this psalm might leave the reader with a sense of repetitiveness or even of monotony: the writer seems to have had one idea in his head and to have gone on about it longer than he need have! But there is much more to it than that. Let us look at its structure.

It has been called a verbal fugue in praise of the law of the Lord. It is composed of twenty-two stanzas, each of eight verses. All stanzas begin with a letter of the Hebrew alphabet and the order is alphabetical—from A to Z as we should say. Close attention has been given to the psalm's structure.

The psalm is a prayer addressed to God; it is a dialogue with God conducted by a devout man of God, a leader whose purpose in writing the psalm was to encourage others in their spiritual life. His own faith was grounded in the law of the Lord. He longed that others should see that this was the way to happiness. Dietrich Bonhoeffer, the great German teacher who was imprisoned and murdered by the Nazis near the end of World War II, regarded Psalm 119 as his favourite. He held the view that the writer of the psalm was a *young* man. Noting verse 9, 'How may a young man lead a clean life?' and verses 99–100, he wrote, 'A young man here asks the question of his life, and he asks it not because of... enthusiasm for the good and noble in general, but because he has experienced the power of the Word of God in his own weakness.'

The psalmist is immensely happy in his discovery of the law of the Lord, its meaning and its relevance to life. Though there is a troubled background to this psalm—the writer has his opponents, and their 'scheming' (v. 23) constantly annoys him—he finds continual delight in God's word. It means more to him than money (v. 14); it tastes sweeter to him than honey (v. 103). From beginning to end of this psalm, the accent is on the sheer joy which study of and obedience to God's law have brought him. In fact the psalm opens with a double beatitude—verses 1 and 2 remind us of our Lord's beatitudes in Matthew 5:3ff. The psalmist's study has not proved restrictive. It has brought him freedom (v. 45). For the writers of the psalms, the law is not a restrictive or oppressive burden, but a joy and delight (see v. 14).

The psalmist uses a wide range of words to tell us what he is thinking about—testimony, precept, statute, commandment, word, decree. It would have been monotonous if he had used only one or two. This is no place to seek to define the particular slant which each word brings to bear on the whole concept. But we must give careful attention to what was in the mind of the writer when he spoke of the 'law' of the Lord. This is the first of four words we shall examine, in order to get to the heart of this psalm.

TO PONDER

'I ate it, and it tasted sweet as honey to me.'
(Ezekiel 3:3)

The LAW *of the* LORD

There is only one verse in this long psalm in which the law, in one or other of its aspects, is not mentioned (v. 76). What is meant by it? The Hebrew word is *torah*, and it means instruction, teaching. In the Old Testament, it is sometimes used in the same sense as we use it in English of a particular law designed to apply to a particular case: in Exodus 12:49, for example: 'The same law will apply both to the native-born and to the alien.' But it is frequently used in a wider sense. We speak of the law of Moses, meaning the range of teaching associated with his name. The widest meaning of the word is that of teaching come from God, through human agency, for the welfare of those who will receive it and live by it—guidance, revelation. This aspect of *torah* is basic to Psalm 119.

To the Hebrews, God's revelation of himself came chiefly through his activity in history. What he did—what he does—indicates what he is like. They never tired of pointing back to the rescue, the 'salvation', performed by God in delivering his people from the tyranny of Egypt. That was 'salvation history'. God's essential being was there manifested—his power, his loving care. 'I am that I am' (Exodus 3:14); our psalmist delights to meditate on the saving name of Yahweh, in creation, in his dealings with Israel, and with himself: 'You have dealt kindly with your servant, fulfilling your word, Lord' (v. 65ff.).

The constancy of God

Behind all that the psalmist writes is the basic concept of the constancy of God. He is just. He keeps his word. He is reliable. In the words of many of the psalms which we have already read, he is a rock. He is as solid as the earth which he has created—'Your faithfulness endures for all generations, and the earth which you have established stands firm' (v. 90). That being so, his decrees can be relied on. 'I know, Lord, that your decrees are just and even in chastening you keep faith with me' (v. 75). 'Your justice is an everlasting justice, and your law is steadfast' (vv. 142; see also Psalm 136 and comment). It is God's steadfastness and justice that evoke our thankfulness and praise.

TO PRAY

Give thanks to the God of heaven.

The COMMANDMENTS *of* GOD

The word 'commandments' introduces us to the personal religion of the writer, for if God is thought of as uttering commands, at the receiving end of those commands must be someone who is obedient to them and responsive to their demands. In Psalm 119 we see a man who is passionately concerned to live a holy life. He wants to be a disciple, and he is prepared to undergo the discipline necessary to that end. 'If only I might hold a steady course, keeping your statutes! Then, if I fixed my eyes on all your commandments, I should never be put to shame' (vv. 5–6). 'I have chosen the path of faithfulness' (v. 30); 'I have obeyed your instruction' (v. 22). 'I say them over, one by one, all the decrees you have announced' (v. 13). 'In the night I remember your name, Lord, and dwell upon your instruction' (v. 55).

The guidance of God

The writer believes that God has planned a path for him—it is his longing to keep to that way. 'Teach me, Lord, the way of your statutes, and in keeping them I shall find my reward' (v. 33). 'Your word is a lamp to my feet, a light on my path' (v. 105). It may be that following in that path will involve suffering, but even that, in the hands of a creative God, will be used to good effect. 'Before I was chastened I went astray, but now I pay heed to your promise' (v. 67). 'How good for me to have been chastened, so that I might be schooled in your statutes!' (v. 71).

Over and over he prays, 'Teach me, Lord'; make me a good listener, receptive, open, obedient. 'Teach me, Lord, the way of your statutes, and in keeping them I shall find my reward' (v. 33; and see vv. 108, 124, 135 etc.). 'Teach, teach, teach,' he prays. This is not merely an academic exercise. It is teaching on the road, direction on the path. Mind and will are both involved. Theory and practice go hand in hand.

If the teaching is learnt and action is taken, what then? There will be a song on his lips. 'Your statutes are the theme of my song throughout my earthly life' (v. 54) or, as the Authorized Version puts it: 'Thy statutes have been my songs in the house of my pilgrimage.' We are reminded of Psalm 40:2–3: 'He raised me out of the miry pit… he set my feet on rock… On my lips he put a new song.' This, surely, is the 'new song' of Revelation, a song of gratitude and worship.

THE NEW SONG

'Worthy is the Lamb who was slain…'
(Revelation 5:12)

MEDITATION

The word 'meditation' is constantly used by our psalmist. Two instances call for comment:

(i) 'I shall meditate on your wonders' (v. 27)—God's action in creation, the miracle of the natural world; God's action in history, especially in his rescue of his people from Egypt; God's dealings with him, the psalmist. All these form the material to which his mind reverts and on which he constantly meditates.

(ii) He has trained himself to pray, to meditate, at all hours. His mind turns to God before dawn, and 'before the midnight watch' his 'eyes are open for meditation on your promise' (v. 148). Paul knew about this habit when he encouraged his Philippian friends to 'fill their thoughts' with things that are 'true, noble, just and pure' (Philippians 4:8). Both psalmist and apostle could join in saying, 'In your commandments I find continuing delight; I love them with all my heart (v. 47).

The Christian disciple, meditating on this psalm, rightly finds its fulfilment in the person of Jesus Christ, himself the way, the truth, and the life (John 14:6). As he learns to abide in Christ, he increasingly finds that Christ is:

(i) **The way:** he prays with the psalmist, 'Teach me, Lord, the way of your statutes'—teach me to know you, for you are the way; keep me on the right path, in step with you.

(ii) **The truth:** the disciple has much to learn and the learning process goes on to the end of his life. In asking God to teach him the truth, he is asking God to teach him to know who is the truth. The disciple who wishes to 'conform to the law of the Lord' is told to 'set his heart on finding *him*' (v. 2), not 'it'!

(iii) **The life:** he wants to 'lead a clean life' (v. 9). 'This is eternal life: to know you the only true God, and Jesus Christ whom you have sent' (John 17:3).

Much of this psalm, interpreted in the light of Jesus as way, truth, and life, can be used as a prayer by the Christian disciple.

A note

Most readers of Psalm 119 have been distressed by what seems to be a self-righteous note in it (see, for example, vv. 22, 30–31, 55–56, 69–70, 99ff. etc.). The writer realized that he was a sinner; but, in fact, he was better than many of his contemporaries, especially those who were seeking to lead him astray. It would have been a false modesty to deny that God's grace was effective in him. We have all experienced occasions when, due entirely to God's mercy, we have escaped from temptation and have won the victory over the tempter. Perhaps the psalmist was not bragging—just being realistic.

PRAYER

Almighty God,
we thank you for the gift of your holy word.
May it be a lantern to our feet, a light to our paths,
and a strength to our lives.
Take us and use us
to love and serve all men
in the power of the Holy Spirit
and in the name of your Son,
Jesus Christ our Lord.

Alternative Service Book 1980, p. 105

Thou art the Way, the Truth, the Life;
Grant us that Way to know,
That Truth to keep, that Life to win,
Whose joys eternal flow.

Bishop G.W. Doane (1799–1859)

PSALM 120

SONG *for* PILGRIMS

All the psalms 120 to 134 inclusive have the superscription 'A Song of the Ascents'. There has been much discussion on what this means. Perhaps the most likely theory is that we have in these psalms a little collection of songs that were used by pilgrims as they ascended the hill in Jerusalem for one of the great festivals. It is hard to see what part this Psalm 120 would have to play in such a 'going up', but overall there is within these psalms a love of Jerusalem, a longing for its welfare, a sense of achievement in reaching it. In 1 Samuel 1:21 it is recorded that 'Elkanah with his whole household went up to make the annual sacrifice to the Lord'. It was a natural phrase for pilgrims to use on such occasions—we note Psalm 122:4—and Psalm 42:4, though it does not use the words 'went up', admirably sets the scene for such occasions.

Personal testimony

Our psalmist begins his little poem with a word of personal testimony. God had answered his prayer in a time of deep distress—his words are similar to those used by the psalmist in 116:1 and in 118:5. The distress was caused by people who had lied and deceived; they had used calumny against him. As a poet—and with a licence which must always be allowed to a poet!—he isolates the tongue as the enemy's instrument and, with a kind of curse, asks it what kind of future it thinks it has. He knows—nothing but sharp arrows and red hot coals (literally, like coals of desert broom). That should teach them a lesson or two!

Verse 5: if, instead of 'wretched is my lot', we had 'wretched was my lot' (and that is all right as a translation), we should here have a little bit of autobiography. Looking back over his life, the psalmist regrets that for so long a time he has had to live away from the holy land, away from fellowship with God's people, away from Jerusalem itself, among people who hated peace. These war-mongers will not even enter into discussion about an amicable agreement. 'I am for peace, but whenever I speak of it, they are for war.' What timeless truth is there! The 'peacemakers' may be 'blessed' (Matthew 5:9), but they are seldom popular with the protagonists. On that note of misery, our psalmist lays aside his pen...

FOR THOUGHT

Peace is a major theme in the Bible. What is meant by it?
Cessation from war? Or more than that?

What does the psalmist mean by it in verses 6 and 7? His own
peace? The peace of Jerusalem (see Psalm 122:6)? Both?
'Peace' in the Hebrew language is 'Shalom', which carries the idea
of being made whole, of living in harmony with God and the
community. It is much more than simply the absence of conflict!

TRAVELLING *from* AFAR

The pilgrims who came, many of them from afar, to worship the Lord in the temple at Jerusalem no doubt encountered dangers on the way. To whom should they look for help? It must have been a temptation to look to one of the gods who were thought to have their homes in the local hills or to the sun or the moon or one of the planets (see 2 Kings 23:5). 'My help,' says our psalmist, 'comes from the Lord' who reigns not over a local hill but who created the universe, 'heaven and earth'. That is a possible translation of these verses, but it is clear that there are other ways of interpreting them. If we have got it roughly right, verse 2 is a strong affirmation of faith in Yahweh himself, and the rest of the psalm is an elaboration on that affirmation.

Dangers of the journey

The dangers are briefly but vividly outlined. Verse 3: there were no roads as we know them for the pilgrim to travel on, only tracks. There was the danger of getting off the track or slipping on the track with the subsequent peril of broken bones—and no medical aid nearby. Verse 5: there was the danger of attack from brigands. Verse 6: there was the danger of sunstroke and of moonstroke (for the moon was often thought of as the cause of disease). The need of a reliable guardian was paramount. That guardian our psalmist finds in the Lord—we note the constant repetition of the word throughout the psalm. Whether the pilgrim was coming or going, the guardian was there (v. 3). Nor was the provision only temporary; it is 'for evermore'. Every emergency is covered. These are, of course, words of faith. This is how the pilgrims are to see things. It is certainly not a blanket assurance that they will never again encounter any problems!

The parallels between the pilgrims engaged in a perilous journey up to Jerusalem and the Christian pilgrim *en route* to heaven are so obvious as to call for no elaboration, though it would be worthwhile to read the psalm again with the preceding paragraph as the guide to our thinking.

THREE PRAYERS

(i)

Be thou my guardian and my guide,
And hear me when I call;
Let not my slippery footsteps slide,
And hold me lest I fall.

Isaac Williams (1802–65)

(ii)

I lift my eyes to the quiet hills
And my heart to the Father's throne;
In all my ways, to the end of days,
The Lord will preserve his own.

Timothy Dudley-Smith (b. 1926)

(iii)

Deepen my trust in your presence, my God, for you seem often
absent or hidden, and I am afraid of what the way will bring.
Deepen my trust.

Jim Cotter, *Towards the City*, Cairns Publications, 1993

The GATES of JERUSALEM

'We have arrived! At last—at long last—after the dangers of uncertain tracks, of brigands, of sunstroke and moonstroke (see Psalm 121), we are here, within your very gates, Jerusalem. Jerusalem, so solid under our feet after those fragile tents, Jerusalem so compact after those wandering tracks (v. 3). When first they mooted the pilgrimage—"Let us go to the house of the Lord"—we rejoiced. Little did we know what we were in for. Now, looking back, was it worth it all? A thousand times, yes. For now, now, we are actually standing within your gates, Jerusalem. It's too good to be true. What a city! With its long association with David, where, in about 1000BC, he installed the Ark, where justice was meted out, where worship was offered up, where in Solomon's day the temple was built—now our feet are standing inside its gates. It's too good to be true.'

Praying for the city

Something like that must have been in the mind of the man who wrote the first five verses of this psalm. At verse 6, the leader of the pilgrims speaks to them all. He bids them pray for its peace, its welfare. He tells them the wording of the prayer they could use: 'May those who love you prosper; peace be within your ramparts and prosperity in your palaces.' And then, as if he were addressing the city itself, on behalf of himself, his brothers and his friends, he says what his prayer will be: 'Peace be within you.' Both for the house of the Lord and the city which contains the house he will constantly pray.

Many years later, Jesus, on his way to the cross, wept over that city of Jerusalem. He yearned for his people, so soon to reject him: 'If only you had known this day the way that leads to peace! But no; it is hidden from your sight' (Luke 19:41, 42). From that sad view of the city, he went (according to Luke's chronology) to the temple and drove out the traders. 'Scripture says, "My house shall be a house of prayer"; but you have made it a bandits' cave' (Luke 19:46). Such magnificence around them! No insight, no life, within them!

The writer of the book of Revelation had a vision of a city, not torn apart by quarrels about racial differences and ambition as is Jerusalem today, but a 'Holy City, new Jerusalem, coming down out of heaven from God', a city where God would dwell with his people, would 'wipe every tear from their eyes', and where there would be 'an end to death, and to mourning and crying and pain, for the old order has passed away' (Revelation 21:1–4). To that day the Christian looks with never-dying hope.

PRAYER

To that hope, the hope of 'the resurrection of the dead, and the life of the world to come,' good Lord, keep us faithful.

PSALM 123

A PERSONAL PSALM

What a charming little psalm this is! There is something personal about it—'I lift my eyes to you' (v. 1). And there is also a group here—'*our* eyes are turned to the Lord' (v. 2); 'show *us* your favour, Lord' (v. 3). The psalmist speaks for a suffering community; he does not specify who were making trouble, but his people are insulted and held up to contempt (v. 4).

It is the metaphors of verse 2 which have aroused my interest—the picture of a slave with his eyes following his master's hand, a slave-girl with her eyes following her mistress's hand. It is a picture of close attention; the eyes are fixed, ready to obey the slightest indication or direction.

Understanding and affection

Of course, everything depends on the character of the master/mistress. If they are brutal, then the attitude of the slave is one of fear, even of terror: that hand might hold a lash! The word 'slave' conjures up for us a picture of harsh domination. But it was not always thus when slavery was part and parcel of the fabric of society. In a big household there would be a wide range of activities, and the work of some slaves would be honourable and responsible. In Exodus 21, there are laws laid down for the right treatment of slaves. For example, when a Hebrew buys a slave, his period of service must not exceed six years; after that he goes free. But Exodus 21:4–6 envisages a situation where the slave's conditions have been such that he has no desire for freedom: 'I am devoted to my master and my wife and children; I do not wish to go free.' The eyes of such a slave have no fear in them when they are fixed on their master's hand. The slave looks for any indication of his master's will, so that he may carry out his directions without hesitation or delay. There is interaction between master and slave based on a relationship not of coercion but of mutual understanding and affection.

Paul delights to speak of himself as the slave of Jesus Christ. That kind of slavery spelt freedom for him. His eyes were fixed on his Lord for the slightest indication of his will. Life for this slave meant glad obedience to his Master. And Jesus himself, of course, gladly took on 'the form of a slave' (Philippians 2:7), seeking to serve, rather than to be served (see Matthew 20:28).

There are two verses of poetry which have meant much to me during my ministry as a bishop in the Church of God. They were written by Charles Hamilton Sorley who, at the age of twenty, was killed in the First World War in 1915. They were sung, at my request, when I took up my work at Bradford (1956), York (1961) and Canterbury (1975). Set to music by Charles Wood, they have moved me greatly, and still do. I share with you two verses for your meditation.

MEDITATION

This sanctuary of my soul
unwitting, I keep white and whole,
unlatched and lit, if thou should'st care
to enter and to tarry there.

With parted lips and outstretched hands
and listening ears thy servant stands.
Call thou early, call thou late,
to thy great service dedicate.

PILGRIMS REJOICING

This is another of the 'songs of the ascents'. We can easily imagine the pilgrims rejoicing in their arrival within the gates of Jerusalem (see Psalm 122). Their leader looks back over their past and the perilous road their forebears had trodden. There had been narrow escapes when foes had attacked them (v. 2), when the raging waters might have carried them away (v. 4), when they might have been a prey in the teeth of their enemies (v. 6), or entrapped like a bird by the fowler (v. 7). (The poet-psalmist is not short on metaphors!) On their recent journey to Jerusalem, they might have succumbed to the temptation to worship one of the hill-gods (see Psalm 121), but they had found their help in the maker of the universe himself.

Temptations

Senior Christian pilgrims today, and others not old enough to come under that category, can look back in their lives to occasions when their feet had almost slipped and they had all but succumbed to some horrific temptation. Over them would have swept 'the raging water'. But in his mercy, the Lord did not leave them a prey for their enemies' teeth. Their help was indeed 'in the name of the Lord, maker of heaven and earth'. It was he who was 'on their side' (v. 1).

Joseph Addison had some such situation in mind when he wrote:

When in the slippery paths of youth
with heedless steps I ran,
thine arm unseen conveyed me safe,
and led me up to man.

Each stage of life has temptations peculiar to itself. There is no exemption from temptation this side of heaven. But always, yes always, there is the presence of 'the Lord, maker of heaven and earth'. 'The Lord of hosts is with us; the God of Jacob is our fortress' (Psalm 46:7, 11). 'Our help is in the name of the Lord'—in his strength, his honour and his purpose.

LET US PRAISE

Now to the One who can keep you from falling and set you
in the presence of his glory, jubilant and above reproach,
to the only God our Saviour, be glory and majesty, power
and authority, through Jesus Christ our Lord, before all time,
now, and for evermore. Amen.
(Jude 24–25)

The UNSHAKEABLE GOD

The psalmists loved to speak of their God as a rock. He cannot be shaken. He stands fast for ever. Here in verse 1 our psalmist says that the followers of such a God have about them rock-like qualities. Those who trust in the Lord cannot be shaken. They stand fast. The Church of God needs such people, stable, steadfast in their commitment to him. The are too many 'fair-weather' Christians, all right when the going is good, but soon knocked over when tragedy strikes.

There is no need for such instability for, although in such a moment they find it hard to believe, the Lord *is* near, surrounding them, rock-like as the mountains surrounding Jerusalem (v. 2). To change the metaphor, the Christian disciple may be surrounded by the thick fog of materialism, the subtle suggestion of the media that the day of Christianity is long past and that if you are 'with it' you cannot maintain a godly stance; but he need not inhale that fog for long. He can breathe deeply the clean, clear air of the Spirit. He need not put his hand to injustice (v. 3) nor 'turn aside into crooked ways' (v. 5). The Lord is near, rock-like as ever.

Hearts in heaven

We remind ourselves that this psalm is one of the songs of the ascents (see Psalm 120). We can envisage the travellers, having survived their journey through slippery tracks, with their feet now on solid rock. They have arrived at the temple at long last. Their feet are on solid ground. Their hearts are in heaven! It is easy to pray the four words with which the psalm ends: 'Peace be on Israel' (v. 5), easy to obey the injunction of Psalm 122:6: 'Pray for the peace of Jerusalem… peace be within your ramparts and prosperity in your palaces'.

What about prayer for the malefactors? The psalmist dismisses them abruptly (v. 5). For him (and it is a divine truth) justice, punishment, even vengeance belong only to the Lord. They are not, in the ultimate sense, our responsibility. Here, it is as if, with that thought, he puts them out of his mind. Can Christians do better? I think they can. I recently came across this prayer by Bishop Oliver Tomkins:

Lord, it is hard to pray for those who ruthlessly destroy others in the belief that their cause justifies it. You manage to love the terrorists, the kidnappers of hostages, the suicide bombers, just as much as you love those whom they kill. I can't manage it. All I feel able to do is to commend them into your keeping. You alone know what to do with them, for Christ's sake, who died for them too.

PRAYER

*Judge eternal, throned in splendour,
Lord of lords and King of kings,
With thy living fire of judgment
Purge this realm of bitter things:
Solace all its wide dominion
With the healing of thy wings.*

H. Scott Holland (1847–1918)

HOME AGAIN

The author's love for Zion shines through this delightful little psalm. The hard days of exile are past. Its fortunes are restored. Its people are back home. There is much laughter and singing. How could they sing the Lord's song in a foreign land (Psalm 137:4)? But now, it is different.

There are neighbouring peoples taking note of Israel's fortunes. People passing through Jerusalem on their trade missions admire the glorious temple buildings, hear the jubilant songs, and say, 'The Lord has done great things for them' (v. 2), and Israel answers back, 'He has indeed' (v. 3). (See Psalm 48, and read Zechariah 8:20–23 to get the full flavour of the situation.)

The second half of the psalm introduces a note of realism and brings us down to earth. There is some hard slogging work to be done if the experience of liberation is to be implemented. When the curse of apartheid was broken in South Africa, people thought that everything would be all right in no time. This has not been the case. Although the government tries hard, the powers of darkness are still at work. Although people work for peace, still in many areas the rule of the gun persists. Our psalmist is convinced that eventually all will be well and truth and justice will prevail, but it may be a long job and it will involve tears and weeping (vv. 5, 6). The Negeb (v. 4) in southern Israel is dry during much of the year, but all of a sudden its water courses fill up and the crops appear. Seeds will produce sheaves. Labour, sweat and tears will issue in victory.

Encouragement for mission

This jubilant yet realistic psalm has a message of great significance and encouragement to those engaged in Christian mission of all kinds. It is well put in Isaiah 55:10–11: 'As the rain and snow come down from the heavens and do not return there without watering the earth, making it produce grain… so it is with my word… it will not return to me empty without accomplishing my purpose and succeeding in the task for which I sent it.' It may be a preacher faithfully pursuing his work; or a translator painfully translating the Bible into a foreign tongue; or a woman bringing a word of comfort to someone in distress or of encouragement to someone depressed. Whoever it is, the assurance is there: 'My word… will not return to me empty.' There is no waste in the economy of God. Faithfulness is all that matters. 'Be faithful till death, and I will give you the crown of life' (Revelation 2:10).

PRAYER

O Lord our God,
make us watchful and keep us faithful
as we await the coming of your Son our Lord;
that, when he shall appear,
he may not find us sleeping in sin
but active in his service;
through Jesus Christ our Lord.

Celebrating Common Prayer, p. 79

A STRANGE PSALM

This is a strange psalm. Although it is one of the 'songs of the ascents', it is difficult to see its relevance to the particular conditions of those going up to worship in the temple; and there seems to be little connection between the opening two verses and the rest of the psalm. The second half of verse 2 has given rise to a wide variety of translations—it remains a problem to scholars. For instance, the NRSV translates the last sentence, 'For he gives sleep to his beloved,' with an alternative footnote, 'Or, "For he provides for his beloved during sleep"'—a rather different idea! For more on verses 3–5 and the blessings inherent in a large family, see Psalm 128.

The closing words of verse 5, 'when confronted by an enemy in court', are a free translation, perhaps giving the impression of a building such as we know where our Justices of the Peace do their work. The psalmist had a very different scene in his mind. In his day, justice was dispensed in an open forum, literally 'in the gate' where there was much coming and going at the entry to the village or city, and where justice could be seen to be done.

Bad attitude

Verses 1 and 2 are concerned with the subject of *work*. The writer is attacking an approach to the subject which leaves God out and which dismisses him as an irrelevance. It is a Godless attitude, a faithless attitude. 'If only,' the psalmist would say, 'if only those who held these views would realize that toil (rising early, going to bed late, toiling for the bread one eats) is in vain.' (Note the threefold 'in vain'.) We can see the furrowed brow, note the rising blood pressure of such a worker. Jesus had such people in mind when at considerable length he tackled the problem of anxiety (about food and drink, clothes, the future): 'How little faith you have! ... Your heavenly Father knows...' (Matthew 6:25–34).

A Godless, faithless attitude to work on the part of the employer may well have repercussions on his attitude to the workers he employs. All too easily, such a person will cease to regard the workers as human beings made, as he himself is, in the image of God. They become mere digits to be used for the financial profit of the employer or his firm. When the Pharisees asked Jesus what was the greatest commandment in the law, he replied that the greatest, the first commandment was 'Love the Lord your God.' The second was 'Love your neighbour as yourself' (Matthew 22:34–40). We note the order of the two commands. We note the relationship of the one to the other. Only those who 'love the Lord' can, in the truest sense, 'love their neighbours'.

PRAYER

Inspire and direct us, O God, to seek and to do your will in all the common affairs of life… in our relations with others, that peace and harmony may prevail; in our work, that truth and justice may be honoured; and in our hearts, that Christ alone may reign there; for the glory of your name.

Adapted from *New Parish Prayers*, edited by Frank Colquhoun, p. 249

PSALM 128

FAMILY LIFE

Psalms 127 and 128 have this in common: they have much to say about family life and the blessing of a large family.

A marriage without children was regarded with horror in biblical times. Rachel's agonized cry, 'Give me sons, or I shall die!' (Genesis 30:1) was echoed by childless women from time immemorial. It was a sign of God's favour when he made 'the woman in a childless house a happy mother of children' (see Psalm 113). To have many sons was to be secure in old age: protection, in a day when there were no social services, would pass from father to son, and the seniors would bask in the sunshine of security provided by the junior members of the family.

Joyful mothers

But there are deeper matters than that of old-age security which these psalms have to teach us. It is *God* who makes the barren woman a joyful mother. 'Sons are a gift *from the Lord*' (127:3). To generate human life is to be in partnership with the divine Creator, and that is a supreme privilege. Procreation is a holy thing. Intercourse is a holy thing. Sex is a holy thing, to be handled with awe and wonder. At the present time, there are lessons to be learnt by Christians who are privileged to take part in a ceremonial meal in a devout Jewish home. On such an occasion, the sheer joy of family life shines through (as food and wine are taken together, Scripture read or recited, all done in an atmosphere at once religious and humorous). In this setting, sex, procreation, family, are hallowed as gifts of God. Such an attitude to life is seen to be not restrictive but positive and creative.

In modern days, other concerns about the creation of big families have to be borne in mind. The world population is growing at an alarming rate and to add to that problem could be an act of irresponsibility. Any social worker will tell us of the misery occasioned by unplanned pregnancies and of the health perils to the mothers concerned. Life lived in 2000AD is much more complicated than life lived in 1000BC!

Yet the psalmist's message is as relevant now as it was three millennia ago. Reverence for God, 'conforming to his ways', respect for one another in a family: these are still the basic ingredients of a true 'home'.

PRAYER

Most gracious Father,
this is our home.
Let your peace rest on it.
Let love abide here,
love of one another,
love of mankind,
love of life itself,
and love of God.
Let us remember
that as many hands build a house,
so many hearts make a home.

New Parish Prayers, edited by Frank Colquhoun, p. 153

ATTACKS *of the* ENEMY

In this psalm the writer is putting into words what he thinks the nation should say to the Lord (v. 1—'Let Israel say…'). This is one of the songs of the ascents; the people going up the hill to Jerusalem are bidden to look back over their long history. They had often been attacked, but God had been victorious, freeing the nation 'from the bonds of the wicked' (v. 4). The psalmist uses his imagination when describing the attacks of the enemy, and the language is so graphic that one wonders whether he himself had at some time suffered the pain of lashes on his back, and whether his vivid metaphor for the scored back arose because he himself had farmed, 'driving long furrows' and churning up the soil.

On verses 5 and following, see my earlier comments on the imprecatory psalms (Introduction, pp. 21–23) and on Psalm 109:8ff. Here the desired vengeance on the writer's enemies is gentler than that in, for example, Psalm 109:8ff., where it is the enemy's children who are to suffer. Here, it is couched in terms which suggest that they come from a country man—the withering grass (v. 6), the mower's hand (v. 7), the pitiful yield.

Words of blessing

We owe the psalmist a small debt. True, he hopes his readers will *not* use the words of blessing in verse 8, but why should we not use them? 'The blessing of the Lord be on you! We bless you in the name of the Lord.' It is strange that they have not found their way into the services of the Church; they have rarely been used liturgically. But they are admirable as a *responsive* greeting. Thus, at the Eucharist, before the congregation exchanges a sign of peace, the celebrant could well greet the worshippers with the words, 'The blessing of the Lord be on you!' and they would reply, 'We bless you in the name of the Lord.'

Again, in a family where father and mother pray with their children, the parents could well greet them with, 'The blessing of the Lord be on you!' and they would reply, 'We bless you in the name of the Lord.' What a good way to begin the day!

ACTION!

'The blessing of the Lord be on you! We bless you in the name of the Lord!' Can we apply these wonderful invocations to those who have 'blessed' us? Perhaps those whose ministry we have cherished, whose books we have read with profit, whose words have nourished our souls? 'The blessing of the Lord be on you!'

CRY *in the* DARK

This is a cry *de profundis*, out of the depths, out of the dark. The darkness is occasioned by the writer's consciousness of his sins; is God at his account-book reckoning them up (v. 3)? There can be no doubt that our psalmist takes sin, personal and national, seriously.

Then a light shines: 'With you is forgiveness' (v. 4). He realizes that God delights to set people free from the sins which had hitherto burdened them and prevented them from enjoying the abundant life which he planned for them. Jeremiah heard God saying, 'I shall forgive their wrongdoing, and their sin I shall call to mind no more' (Jeremiah 31:34). And Jesus—forgiveness was at the centre of his teaching. It was at the heart of the prayer which he taught his desciples: 'Forgive us the wrong we have done, as we have forgiven those who have wronged us' (Matthew 6:12). Jesus knew that if we do not forgive those who have injured us, we injure *ourselves*, for a kind of callus grows over our hearts which stops us from receiving God's forgiveness. The after-effects of such forgiveness are astonishing. An inner serenity, peace of heart and mind, issue from a right relationship with God and with our neighbours.

Power to deliver

Our psalmist put it admirably: 'In the Lord is love unfailing, and great is his power to deliver' (v. 7). No longer is he in the depths of despair. Morning has broken. Everything looks different in the light of God's forgiveness. He has 'power' to deliver.

The picture of the watchman eagerly awaiting the first streaks of dawn is good. Darkness spelt danger for the citizens whom he was guarding. Light spelt safety. The forgiveness of God was as sure as the coming of the new day. That gave the psalmist a sense of serenity and of hope. Like the dawn driving away the night, the coming of the Lord dismisses his despair.

The focus of this psalm is both personal—'I wait for the Lord... I put my hope in his word' (v. 5)—and national—'Let Israel look for the Lord' (v. 7); 'He alone will set Israel free...' (v. 8). As in other 'songs of the ascents', there is the dual concern. The writers care for the *nation* as well as for themselves, so Psalm 128 ends with 'Peace be on Israel', and Psalm 131 with 'Israel, hope in the Lord...'

TO PONDER

In Psalm 123 we had the picture of slaves looking to their masters, 'awaiting his favour' and the indications of his will. In this psalm we have the picture of the psalmist eagerly waiting for the Lord with a hope as keen as that of a watchman awaiting the first streaks of dawn. With such a hope, how can we despair?

'My soul waits for the Lord. For in the Lord is love unfailing.'

A STRANGE LITTLE PSALM

Two questions suggest themselves as we look at this strange little psalm, and to neither can a firm answer be given.

(i) Was it written by a woman? The writer seems to know what he/she is talking about!

(ii) Is it a fragment from a longer psalm? It seems hardly complete in itself.

Though we shall never know the answer to these questions, the psalm deserves a careful look.

Verse 1: I do not regard this verse as self-congratulatory in the wrong sense. A modern equivalent might run something like this: 'I am just an ordinary lay man/woman in the Church. My name never appears in the Church papers. I have nothing to boast about. I take my share in the worship and work of the Church. I seek to bear my Christian witness in my business and in my social contacts.' In people like this the Church's work is done and God is glorified.

Verse 2: 'But I am calm and quiet, like a weaned child clinging to its mother'—what a homely image of the anxious, crying baby suddenly finding peace and security at its mother's breast! In the book of Isaiah there are four little sketches of the Servant of the Lord (Isaiah 42:1–9; 49:1–6; 50:4–9; 52:14—53:12). Christians have seen in them a kind of picture-in-advance of Jesus, the Servant-Son of God. In the first of these, it is said of him that 'he will not shout or raise his voice, or make himself heard in the street'. He does not need to make a noise. His quietness is self-authenticating. Further, 'He will not break a crushed reed or snuff out a smouldering wick.' Tenderness marks his actions. Again, 'He will never falter or be crushed.' There is a toughness about him which is notable, and which itself derives from his quietness and his tenderness.

Afraid of silence?

'Calm and quiet,' said our psalmist. Quiet, tender, tough, said Isaiah and, in a lovely couplet, put it well: 'In calm detachment lies your safety, your strength in quiet trust' (Isaiah 30:15). Our present-day society seems frightened of silence—the radio or television must always be on. It is frightened of pause—it must always be in action, even if action leads to nothing. So there are breakdowns, burn-outs, and the psychiatrist must be called in. Here is the opportunity for the ministry of the Christian disciple if she/he has learnt to be 'calm and quiet'. People in need of tender love and care will never come to us if we are always talking, rarely listening, never 'calm and quiet'.

SILENCE

In silence we meditate on the motherliness of God. 'As a mother comforts her son so shall I myself comfort you' (Isaiah 66:13).

God, help me to be calm and quiet.
Make me a good listener.
Give me quietness, tenderness, toughness,
through Jesus Christ, the Servant-Son.

The ARK of the LORD

There are two passages from the books of Samuel which must be read if we are to understand this psalm:

(i) 2 Samuel 7:1–16 provides the context of verses 1–5. We are called to 'remember' David in his adversity, and the solemn oath which he swore. David is well established in his home after defeating his enemies. It seems wrong to him that he should be living in dignified quarters while the Ark, which symbolizes the awesome presence of God, is housed in a tent. Surely he must erect a building more worthy of God? He shares his anxiety with Nathan the prophet, who passes on to him a message which he has received from the Lord. God is concerned about a building project in his own mind—that of building up David's line and the security of his people! As to the building of a temple and a worthy place in which to put the Ark, that was not to be David's task. He had been a man of war. His son, Solomon, the wise man of peace, would carry out what David had in mind.

(ii) 1 Samuel 6:21—7:2 is the context for verses 6–8. The Ark, after a long period of wandering, had eventually come to reside in Kiriath-jearim. This is Jaar, mentioned in verse 6 of our psalm (Ephrathah is Bethlehem, David's birthplace).

What was this Ark? We know what it looked like. It was a wooden box, measuring some 45 x 27 x 27 inches, overlaid with gold, surmounted by two cherubim and carried on two gold poles (Exodus 25:10ff.). What was its purpose? It was the most sacred symbol of God's awesome presence. Too sacred to be touched by human hands (read the story of what happened to poor Uzzah when he, apparently with good intent, touched it: 2 Samuel 6:1–8), it had a mystique all its own. When Solomon's temple came to be built, it was kept in the Holy of Holies where even the priests were not allowed to enter, the only exception being the high priest himself—and that only once a year.

In verses 6–10 we hear the voice of the worshippers as the Ark is installed in its place with joy and solemnity. No more journeyings— it has come to rest where it rightly belongs. David's desire has been fulfilled.

Covenant with the people

And so has God's desire been fulfilled. David's line will be established. God is entering into an agreement, a covenant (v. 12), with his people. At last God is at home in Zion (vv. 13–14). Here he will dwell, surrounded by priests and loyal servants. When David has gone, his successor (God's anointed one, God's Messiah) will be crowned with a shining crown, enlightened with a lamp prepared by God himself (vv. 17–18).

In Israel's history books, the story of David, the shepherd-boy who became king, is told in detail. In spite of his lapses—the story of his adultery with Bathsheba and the murder of Uriah her husband is presented with frankness (2 Samuel 11)—he became the model of a coming King on whom the people pinned their hope, a Messiah who would ensure the stability and prosperity of his people. But human beings are all fallible, liable to break the covenant relationship which God longs to maintain with his people. It was of David's line that Jesus came (Matthew 1:17). As Paul pointed out, God's Son 'on the human level... was a descendant of David' (Romans 1:4).

So this psalm brings us back to David and his desire to build a temple, to God and his desire to build a people in a covenant relationship with himself, the installation of the Ark in the most holy place of Israel's worshipping; and forward to the maintenance of David's line which Christians believe found its fulfilment in Jesus.

THANKSGIVING

Thank God for his desire to enter into agreements with his people—covenants of closeness. When next you join in Eucharistic worship, thank him specially for the new covenant and for his Son's blood 'shed for you and for many'.

COMMUNITY *of* WORSHIP

What community did the writer have in mind when he wrote this psalm? It is one of the 'songs of the ascents'. Possibly he was surprised and delighted at the unity which he noted in those who came up to the festival in Jerusalem (v. 1). They had come from different countries. They had widely differing backgrounds. But they were one in their desire to worship the God of Israel. In this they were a band of brothers. It was as refreshing as if the dew of snow-capped Hermon in the north were falling on the parched areas in the south (v. 3).

Verse 2: the psalmist is alluding to the situation described in Leviticus 8:12, when Moses consecrated Aaron by pouring the anointing oil on his head.

From the beginning of the Christian movement, oil has been widely used. Mark records that when Jesus sent out the Twelve on their journey, they 'anointed many sick people with oil and cured them' (Mark 6:13). James bids anyone who is ill to 'send for the elders of the church to pray over him and anoint him with oil in the name of the Lord…' (James 5:14). Oil symbolized Christ's presence to heal, and has been part of the rites of baptism, confirmation and ordination in many branches of the Church (as well as in the coronation of sovereigns). It speaks of warmth and comfort and health and is increasingly used in informal services of healing today.

Unity for mission

The World Council of Churches recently celebrated the fiftieth year of its inception. Much has happened in the sphere of Church unity during that half-century. If at times progress has been slow at the level of agreement arising out of official consultations, immense progress has occurred at the grass-root levels of parish and diocese. There, ordinary worshippers have got to know one another, to pray together, to evangelize together. Brothers and sisters in Christ have discovered a unity which has surprised them. We may expect further progress at that level, while we continue to pray for courageous thinking and leadership from the 'officials' of the churches. At the point of unity, 'there the Lord bestows his blessing' (v. 3).

A QUOTATION

St Aelred was a twelfth-century abbot of Rievaulx in Yorkshire.
Sensitive, gentle, holy, he drew around him men of similar
character to his own, and did much to humanize the Cistercian
order. He wrote:

'The day before yesterday I was walking around the cloister of the
monastery, the brethren were sitting around forming as it were a
most loving crown. In the multitude I found no one whom I did not
love and by whom I felt sure I was not loved. I was filled with such
joy that it surpassed all the delights of the world. I felt my spirit
transfused into all and the affection of all to have passed into me,
so that I could say with the prophet: Behold how good and pleasant
it is for brothers to dwell together in unity.'

A QUESTION

What would happen if the quotation were printed at the head of
your parochial church council agenda (or other group) and ten
minutes of silence were allowed for meditation on it before
proceeding with the business of the meeting?

DIALOGUE *on* MINISTRY

We have seen that these 'songs of the ascents' (of which this is the last), short as most of them are, have raised issues of considerable importance. For example, Psalm 127 invites us to consider the matter of work, 128 the matter of family, 133 that of unity. This psalm (134) touches on ministry. It is a little piece of dialogue.

The pilgrims on their way to the temple (see Psalm 120) are the speakers of verses 1 and 2. They are addressing the priests, the 'servants' of the Lord who minister constantly. The pilgrims are about to leave for their homes. The priests will remain, a rota of them doing night duty in the temple. The pilgrims want to leave the priests with a word of encouragement: go on serving, go on ministering, go on praying ('lift up your hands'), go on blessing.

With clear insight, these lay men and women fasten on the essential work of the ministry: it is God-centred, it is centred in the sanctuary, it is prayerful.

A weighty blessing

The priests are the speakers in verse 3. They respond to the encouragement of the laity, saying, 'May the Lord... bless you' as you leave Zion (Jerusalem) and go on your ways. There is weight in this blessing, for it is given in the name of the 'maker of heaven and earth'—the same phrase is used in Psalm 124:8. There is much warmth in this interchange of greetings. To 'minister... in the house of the Lord' is an awesome responsibility and a huge privilege. They 'bless' the people; the people 'bless' them. There is a sense of interdependence.

The selection and training of aspirants to the ordained ministry is crucial to the future well-being of the Church. What are the essential questions to be asked of candidates or, for that matter, young ministers? 'Are they competent and literate? Are they able to administer a parish and are they at home with the mechanics of running it? Are they in touch with a psychiatrist who will help them with personality problems?' Or: 'Have they the makings of a man or woman of prayer? Do they love their Master? What do they consider to be the heart of the Christian faith and message?' The practicalities of organization they can learn along the way. But are there (necessarily in elementary form) faith, a concern for doctrine, prayer, at the centre of the young leader's being? These are the things that matter.

PRAYER

Lord of the Church and Saviour of all, call to the Church's ministry those whom you want, and grant them the gifts which they need: open their minds to truth and their hearts to love, strengthen their wills to serve and their bodies to endure, keep printed in their remembrance how great a treasure is committed to their charge, through Jesus Christ our Lord.

Bishop Oliver Tomkins, *Asking God*, p. 32

PSALM 135

A CHEERFUL PSALM

This is a cheerful psalm, a psalm of praise, wide in its outreach, confident in the God with whose nature and purpose it is concerned. Let us watch the psalmist at work.

In verses 1–4 he encourages the ministers in the temple to get on with their essential work of leading the worship and praise of the people.

In verse 5 we find the only personal reference to the psalmist's own faith in his Lord's power—'I know...'

In verses 5–7, he pays his tribute to God's power seen in nature, while in verses 8–14 he pays his tribute to God's power as seen in the history of Israel and in rescuing the people from Egypt—he is a God of justice and compassion (v. 14).

In verses 15–18 there are words of scorn directed at 'the gods of the nations', words which are almost identical with Psalm 115:4–8. Both psalmists end the passages with the stinging words that the makers of those gods 'become like them'—senseless and useless.

In verses 19 and 20 the wording is again similar to Psalm 115:12–13: three groups are called on to 'bless the Lord': (i) all the people, the 'house of Israel'; (ii) the priestly class, the 'house of Aaron', with the 'house of Levi' functioning under Aaronic supervision; (iii) 'you that fear the Lord', a group which would include godly Gentiles who were learning to reverence Israel's God and to worship him (see Isaiah 56:1–8). They were known as 'God-fearers' or, less colourfully, 'proselytes'. They, too, are called to 'bless the Lord'.

A centre of blessing

In verse 21, it is 'from Zion' that the Lord is blessed by these groups, it is 'in Jerusalem' that he dwells. There is his temple. There is the Ark, the sacred reminder of God's unbreakable covenant with his people. There God blesses his people. There they bless him.

In the book of the prophet Ezekiel, there is a remarkable passage in which the prophet has a vision of water emanating from the temple in ever-increasing depth and with ever-widening blessing and healing to the nations (Ezekiel 47:1–12). Barren areas are irrigated. Even the Dead Sea is sweetened. Fruitful trees grow up with never-fading leaves—'their fruit is for food and their leaves for healing'. Our psalmist would have been well content with that vision of Ezekiel. For in the mind of God, Jerusalem was to be a centre of blessing for all nations, and Israel was to be the agent of that blessing.

MEDITATION

The aged Simeon found the fulfilment of God's purpose when in Jerusalem he took the baby Jesus in his arms, 'a light that will bring revelation to the Gentiles and glory to your people Israel'
(Luke 2:32).

PSALM 136

Everlasting Love

As the refrain 'for his love endures for ever' occurs twenty-six times in this psalm, we should look at it closely. The Revised English Bible translates the Hebrew as 'love'; so does the Jerusalem Bible and the Good News Bible. The Revised Standard Version has 'steadfast love'; the Authorized Version has 'mercy'. Artur Weiser in his commentary has, more daringly, 'grace'. The Hebrew word (*chesed*) occurs very frequently in the Old Testament when the writers seek to express God's dealings with and his attitude to his creatures, especially to those who are lowly or needy or miserable.

The quality of God's relationship to his people is shown supremely in his redemption of his people from Egyptian tyranny, and in his preservation of them in times of danger. Often it has about it a strong flavour of God's fidelity to the covenant which he has established with them. This covenant, or 'agreement', pledged them to be 'his people', and pledged him to be 'their God', the recipients of his *chesed*.

What a rich word! Its depth of meaning should restrain us from rattling off the refrain thoughtlessly when reciting the psalm. It is seen in the creation of the universe (vv. 1–9), in the history of God's people (vv. 10–24), and in his universal generosity to all humankind (v. 25). The God of heaven (v. 26) stoops down in grace.

Choir and people

Clearly, this psalm was composed to be sung antiphonally, the temple choir singing the first line of each couplet and the people responding with the refrain. In modern times the Taizé community is showing us how profitable such antiphonal worship can be—the repetition of the refrain, so far from being soporific, keeps the congregation on the alert. The worship becomes, in a deep sense, 'corporate', choir and people combining to sing God's praise. It would be possible for a group of people to use this psalm antiphonally in worship, or indeed to compose a similar one with present-day items of thanksgiving and intercession.

PRAYER

In July 1998 bishops from all over the world met in Canterbury for
the Lambeth Conference. In the opening service of Eucharistic
worship, words from the Kenyan rite were used, which express
God's involvement with his people in similar terms to those of
Psalm 136:

'It is right and our delight to give you thanks and praise,
great Father, living God, supreme over the world,
Creator, Provider, Saviour and Giver.
From a wandering nomad you created your family;
for a burdened people you raised up a leader;
for a confused nation you chose a king;
for a rebellious crowd you sent your prophets.

In these last days you sent us your Son, your perfect image,
bringing your kingdom, revealing your will, dying, rising, reigning,
rescuing your people for yourself. Through him you have poured
out your Holy Spirit, filling us with light and life. And now we give
you thanks...'

Let us use this prayer from the Kenyan rite and combine it with a
prayer for God's church in Africa.

PATHOS & PASSION

It is impossible to read this psalm carefully without being moved by its pathos and passion. Nor is it difficult to sketch the historical situation which gave rise to this very human cry of agony. Jerusalem, this city dearly loved by the psalmist and his friends, was in ruins, destroyed in 587BC. The flower of its citizens, our psalmist among them, had been deported to Babylon. Now they were back home again, surveying the scene of desolation. They could do little but indulge in bitter memories of what happened to them in their captivity. The opening four verses tell the story.

Sacred songs

They were sitting one day by a river, singing. Were they singing one of the psalms with which we are familiar? Psalm 46, perhaps: 'There is a river whose streams bring joy to the city of God... God is in her midst; she will not be overthrown.' Or 48: 'Great is the Lord... His holy mountain is fair and lofty, the joy of the whole earth. The mountain of Zion...' As they sang their sacred songs, they thought of their separation from their homeland. They thought of their separation from the temple with its Ark which reminded them of the presence of God and of his covenant-relationship with his people (see Psalm 136). How could they sing the Lord's song in a foreign land? The song died on their lips. The situation was made worse by the mocking of their captors—'Sing us one of your little ditties!' How could they? It would be casting pearls before swine. They could only relapse into a dreadful silence. The psalmist would prefer his hand to wither and his tongue to cleave to the roof of his mouth than to reply to the blasphemous invitation of those who mocked him (vv. 5–6). Jerusalem was his chief joy—nothing could surpass it.

Only when we have entered into the bitterness of this cry of agony, a bitterness which itself sprang from the deeps of the writer's religion, can we begin to understand the passionate rage and hatred of verses 7–9.

Such bitterness is not assuaged by ignoring it or covering it up. In some ways it needs to be expressed, perhaps best of all, as here, in the context of a cry to God for justice. The psalmist tells God that he would congratulate the one who dashed his persecutors' babies against a rock. The language is shocking and revolting. But these appalling words are expressed in the context of faith in the God who is Judge of all: of us, and of our enemies. Vengeance is *his*, but so is mercy. He is Judge, and Saviour.

PRAYER

From the corroding memories of past events,
good Lord, deliver us.
In the forgiving of those who malign us,
good Lord, help us.

RINGING *with* ASSURANCE

This psalm rings with the assurance of God's faithfulness, his trust-worthiness. It would seem that the writer is in some foreign country —he bows down, not in God's 'holy temple', but towards it (v. 2). His position is like that of Daniel who, in a foreign land and under direct threat, went into his house and knelt down three times a day in a roof-chamber whose windows opened towards Jerusalem. There he offered his prayers and praises (Daniel 6:10). There is something of a parallel in the action of a devout Muslim who, wherever he may be, prostrates himself facing the sacred city of Mecca. In the presence of gods which are no God, our psalmist sings his psalms to Yahweh.

He longs that 'all the kings of the earth', the potentates of the laws in which he lived out his life, should praise his God, hear his words, learn his ways, see his glory, glimpse his care of the insignificant (vv. 4–6). Like the author of Psalm 119, he is deeply convinced of the rock-like constancy of God. See also the refrain of Psalm 136—his love, his constancy, his tenacity of purpose 'endure for ever'.

God's purposes

To this divine constancy he bears his personal testimony in verses 7 and 8. In the vicissitudes of life, he is 'preserved', 'saved', the object of an 'enduring' love. Whatever happens to him, he is not 'abandoned'. God has a purpose for him which God himself is determined to see through to the end; he has set his hand to achieving it and he will not look back. The Christian knows what that purpose is, namely, that he should share the likeness of God's Son (Romans 8:29). The achievement of that purpose may be long in coming, indeed it will be life-long, and the clay of our character may prove to be difficult in the hand of the Potter; but, so far as God is concerned, the Christian disciple may be assured of his faithfulness. His constant love will never let him go.

The psalmist bowed down towards God's holy temple. The Christian bows down, in contemplation and adoration, towards Christ's holy cross. With eyes fixed on that, he can make his own the first verse of George Matheson's hymn:

O Love that wilt not let me go,
I rest my weary soul on thee;
I give thee back the life I owe,
that in thine ocean depth its flow
may richer, fuller be.

PRAYER

Make the verse your own. In the second line, pray it as it is, if you
are physically or mentally weary, or if you are weary of life as it
has previously been and you want to start again. If you are not
weary, substitute for 'weary' a word that describes your present
state, for example 'joyful' or 'sinful' or 'anxious' or 'wistful' or
'needy'. Then complete the verse, using it as your own prayer.
It is a prayer which God will love to hear.

PSALM 139

INESCAPABLE GOD

'You know me' (v. 1). 'You know me' (v. 2). 'You know me through and through' (v. 14). This is the theme of this astonishing psalm. The theme is elaborated in great detail. It is a mystery beyond human grasp (vv. 6, 17–18), but none the less true for that. Wherever the psalmist journeys (v. 3), whatever his speech (v. 4), all is known to God. He cannot escape from God—God is in heaven and in Sheol (the grave, v. 8), in the East and beyond the Western sea (vv. 9–10), in the darkness of the night as well as the brightness of the day (vv. 11–12). Before his birth, from the moment of his conception, God is there, fashioning his life 'before it had come into being' (v. 16).

'Almighty God,' we pray in the opening prayer of the Eucharist, 'to whom all hearts are open, all desires known, and from whom no secrets are hidden'. The collect owes much to the psalm. As you join in that prayer, in what tone do you say it? Is there about it a touch of anxiety—all things 'bare and exposed to the eyes of him to whom we must render account' (Hebrews 4:13)? Or is there more than a touch of anxiety—perhaps sheer fear? Or is there a touch, or more than a touch, of infinite relief? God knows me through and through; I cannot hide from God, nor would I.

It all depends on what we think God is like. If—perhaps from some idea of him given to us in childhood and never fully thrown off—we think of him as something of a tyrant, ready to snatch the carpet from under our feet, then the idea of an all-knowing God is enough to scare the wits out of us. If, on the other hand, we have come to think of God as essentially love and whose design for us is to make us like his Son, then the concept is one of immense comfort and assurance (see Psalm 138). 'You know me through and through.' Where can we escape from his Spirit, where flee from his presence (v. 7)? We cannot. Thanks be to God.

Awe and wonder

We know far more about the beginnings of human life than did this psalmist, yet the more we know, the greater is the mystery of God's foreknowledge and of his purpose. We share the writer's sense of awe and wonder.

In his book *The Return of the Prodigal Son*, Henri Nouwen has a section entitled 'The Heart of God'. In it he writes:

> *There is no doubt… about the father's heart. His heart goes out to both of his sons; he loves them both; he hopes to see them together as brothers around the same table; he wants them to experience that, different as they are, they belong to the same household and are children of the same father. As I let all this sink in, I see how the story of the father and his lost sons powerfully affirms that it was not I who chose God, God chose me. From all eternity we are hidden 'in the shadow of God's hand' and 'engraved on his palm'. Before any human being touches us, 'God forms us in secret' and 'textures us' in the depth of the earth, and before any human being decides about us, God 'knits us together in a mother's womb'. He loves us with a 'first' love, an unlimited, unconditional love (pp. 105–106).*

Verses 19–22 are strangely interruptive. Have they crept in from some other source, perhaps by a scribe's error? Their tone is similar to that of passages in several of the surrounding psalms, of course: an expression of hatred and contempt for God's enemies (and the psalmist's persecutors). On the other hand, it may be that the thoughts in verses 1 and 2, picked up in the final verses, caused him to confess these feelings of hatred and bitterness. If God already *knew* them, then he could ensure that they would not lead on to a 'path that grieved' him (v. 24).

PRAYER

Examine me, God, and know my mind;
test me and understand my anxious thoughts;
watch lest I follow any path that grieves you;
lead me in the everlasting way.

HIDDEN TRAPS

It is unlikely that many people who read this commentary will have had an experience such as that which our psalmist had. He seems to have been a frightened man, afraid of physical hurt, of being in the clutches of wicked people who use violence to get their way. They set hidden traps, spread their nets and lay snares (vv. 1–5). The psalmist immediately reminds himself of his faithful God (vv. 6–8), who will hear his plea, shield his head and 'frustrate the desires of the wicked'. Yet the context is of fear and hurt, of vulnerability to evil words and actions.

If there are readers with an experience like this, it may well be that their first reaction was that of the psalmist in verses 9–11: vengeance is sweet. God, pay them out in their own coin! It is to be hoped that, in the light of our Lord's command to 'love your enemies and pray for your persecutors; only so can you be children of your heavenly Father...' (Matthew 5:44–45), they might rise above that first reaction and let grace prevail.

It is more likely that many readers know what it is, not to experience fear of physical hurt, but to know the devastation which comes from having their characters torn to shreds by the spread of rumours which are wholly false. Somebody has it in for them, and starts a rumour on its rounds of mischief. 'Of course, my dear,' so the talk begins, 'I wouldn't tell a soul but you, but I did hear that he's not up to much. I even heard... That is, of course, between you and me...' 'The tongue is a fire... its flames are fed by hell,' warned James in his letter; 'the tongue... is small, but its pretensions are great' (James 3:6, 5).

Close to home

Read like this, this psalm is no longer remote. It strikes uncomfortably close to experiences which come to most of us at some point in our lives. 'Speed can kill,' say the posters on the roads. 'Gossip can kill' is a warning all of us should heed.

What we have so far said has had a negative note to it. Paul—as usual—has something positive to say about what proceeds from our mouths. Writing to the Colossians, he says, 'Let your words always be gracious, never insipid; learn how best to respond to each person you meet' (4:6). 'Never insipid'—Moffatt gives a translation which is nearer to the original: 'Let your talk always have a saving salt of grace about it'—talk which leads to higher things, and so responds to human need.

PRAYER

Lord, set a guard on my mouth; keep watch at the door of my lips.
(Psalm 141:3)

Take my lips, and let them be
Filled with messages from thee.

Frances R. Havergal (1836–79)

PRAYERS RISING

This is a psalm about prayer. The writer calls upon God (v. 1), his eyes are fixed on God (v. 8), in expectation of his help. Just as the sweet scent of incense rose to God in the daily offerings of sacrificed beasts, so do his prayers go up to God (v. 2a). The lifting up of his hands (v. 2b)—the normal Jewish posture of prayer—may be an echo here of the story in Exodus 17:8–13, where the hands of Moses were kept uplifted by Aaron and Hur so that the enemy might be defeated. Once the hands were lowered, Amalek prevailed.

Verses 5–7 are notoriously difficult. The Hebrew seems to be corrupt. One has only to consult different translations to see how the scholars have wrestled with the text. The result of their wrestlings is seen in translations of great variety. The best scholars admit defeat. Perhaps the chaotic state of the text reflects a chaos in the mind of the poet-psalmist—he is struggling with his prayers (don't we all?). Even that giant of a Christian, Paul, admits that 'we do not even know how we ought to pray'. He confesses that his prayers are some-times 'inarticulate groans'. What is he to do? Give up praying? Never! To do so would be to forget the ever-near presence of the Holy Spirit who, as it were, takes these wordless groanings and interprets them in the ears of the Father (Romans 8:26–30). Martin Luther got close to Paul's thoughts when he wrote, 'A Christian is always praying... and even a little sigh is a great and mighty prayer.'

Dear to God

This is immensely encouraging. 'My eyes are fixed on you, Lord' (v. 8). That seems to be the clue. Even the heart's desire is dear to God, inexpressible though that desire is. 'If ever desiring, then ever pray-ing,' wrote Augustine.

Let us be very practical here. We have a friend. He is in deep trouble, of body or mind or spirit. We are much concerned about him. What precisely does he need? We do not know. We certainly cannot express it in words. What we do know is that God loves him—loves him dearly. We do, too. With him in our mind, in silence, we share in the strong, wise loving of God. We hold him in that love. That, wordless though it is, is prayer—and prayer that avails.

TO PONDER

Prayer is the soul's sincere desire,
Uttered or unexpressed,
The motion of a hidden fire
That trembles in the breast.

From James Montgomery, *What is Prayer?*

BESET *with* TROUBLES

Our psalmist is beset with troubles. He is faint-hearted (v. 3), friend-less and dreadfully alone (v. 4), harassed (v. 6), and imprisoned (v. 7) not, perhaps, in the literal sense of that word, but depressed with the feeling that he will never get free from his inhibitions.

But at least he knows where to go in his grief—to the Lord (v. 1); to him he can 'unfold' his troubles. Did he know of another man in trouble, by name Hezekiah? That king had received a letter from the powerful king Sennacherib threatening the annihilation of his people if he, Hezekiah, did not submit to his insolent threats. Other nations had crumbled before the Assyrian onslaught—why should Hezekiah think that his God, Yahweh, would deliver Israel from his clutches? It was a vicious letter. 'Hezekiah,' so the story runs, 'received the letter from the messengers and, having read it, he went up to the temple and spread it out before the Lord with this prayer...' (Isaiah 37: 14–15). He 'unfolded' his troubles, spread them out before the Lord: let him deal with Sennacherib!

The psalmist's spirit may be faint within him. His faith may be small as a grain of mustard seed, but he knows that God is there. 'You are there to watch over my steps' (v. 3). 'You are my refuge; you are my portion in the land of the living' (v. 5).

Silent comfort

The presence of another person when in trouble is often of more value than a spate of words. A friend of mine who suffered from depression wrote of his deepest need when he was at his worst. It was the need, not of phone calls or letters or advice to 'snap out of it'; it was the need for the presence of someone with him. As someone once said to a doctor, 'Don't just say something. Sit there!'

The heirs of Eastern cultures are more sensitive in this matter than are we talkative Westerners. When there has been a bereavement in, let us say, an Indian or Pakistani village, the neighbours of the bereaved relatives will come and sit, often for long periods of time, with the mourners. No words are uttered. Their presence is enough to convey sympathy and to spread comfort. 'You are there,' said the psalmist. That was enough to bring confidence and even a measure of hope. There is power in shared silence.

'Even were I to walk through a valley of deepest darkness I should fear no harm, for you are with me,' said another psalmist (Psalm 23:4). The companionship of God is enough.

PRAYER

'I unfold my troubles in his presence.'

Jesu, thou joy of loving hearts,
Thou fount of life, thou light of men!
From the best bliss that earth imparts
We turn unfilled to thee again.

R. Palmer (1808–87)

PSALM 143

The POINT *of* DESPAIR

Here is a man in deep trouble. Someone has dealt him a dirty blow—
'An enemy has hunted me down and crushed me underfoot' (v. 3).
That has brought him to the point of despair (v. 4). There is a touch
of vindictiveness in his reaction (v. 12).

But there are hopeful and positive signs as he faces his crisis. His
memory is unimpaired; that is a cause for thanksgiving. He looks
back over his past life with gratitude for all God has done. His mind
is well stored, and he recalls the times when he has appreciated the
beauty of nature (a summer holiday? a bunch of flowers? a butterfly?)
(v. 5). Best of all, he has not lost his thirst for God (v. 6). He lets his
imagination run: it is winter and he sees a ploughed field, its clods
open to anything that comes—rain, frost, snow, ice, sunshine. He
feels like that and, as he thinks, he finds himself acting out the
picture; he lifts his outspread hands to God. (Why not try that out in
your room when you are praying?)

The coming morning

It has been dark as night (v. 7). But morning always follows night. He
dares to hope that 'in the morning' God will let him know of his
smile (v. 8). So he turns to prayer—and in doing so, gives us four
little gems which we can make our own:

(i) 'Show me the way that I must take' (v. 8b)—a prayer for guidance.

(ii) 'Deliver me... from my enemies (v. 9)—a prayer for rescue
from anything which gets him down.

(iii) 'Teach me to do your will' (v. 10—a prayer for fuller entry into
the meaning of that central part of the Lord's prayer, 'Thy will be
done, thy kingdom come'.

(iv) 'Revive me, Lord' (v. 11)—a prayer for daily renewal.

A hint for the next four days: take these prayers and make them your
own—one each day. Use it in the morning. Use it before going to
sleep. If you can, use it on and off during the day. Let your mind
revert to it as often as possible. On the fifth day, glance back over all

four prayers. Have you made them your own? What difference has this kind of praying made to you?

A WARNING

There is a second part to the third of the four prayers mentioned above: 'By your gracious spirit guide me on level ground' (v. 10b). Here is a warning to Christians of all ages and at all stages of their spiritual pilgrimage: don't be cocky or over-confident in yourself. Look out. You can easily miss your footing, trip up, and deny your Master or injure one of his children. 'If you think you are standing firm, take care, or you may fall' (1 Corinthians 10:12).

Let not my slippery footsteps slide,
And hold me lest I fall.

Isaac Williams (1802–65)

WARRIOR & PATRIOT

The writer of this psalm is a warrior who sees his victory in battle as a sign of God's approval. His nation is now secure (vv. 1–2). He is a patriot, whose vision for his country is one of prosperity in home (v. 12) and field (vv. 13–14)—all under the smile of God.

At the same time, he is conscious of the fragility of human beings and of the brevity of their lives (vv. 3–4). It is a familiar theme in the psalms (see, for example, Psalm 49 and 103:14–16)—and in other biblical writings. It is amplified in a moving passage in the Apocrypha (see Ecclesiasticus 18:8–14). *Because* human life is brief and fragile, 'the Lord is patient with people; that is why he lavishes his mercy on them'. *Memento mori*, 'remember you must die', were words seen frequently in previous centuries, often illustrated by the representation of a skull. A modern generation prefers not to remember, and to brush aside the reality of death and its nearness.

Our psalmist's consciousness of the nearness of death is linked specifically to the treachery of some fellow human beings 'whose every word is worthless, whose every oath is false' (note the repetition in verses 8 and 11). He looks to God for rescue and, in highly poetic language, bids him 'part the heavens and come down... Discharge your lightning flashes... and send your arrows humming' (vv. 5, 6). God had done it for David, let him do it again! (v. 10).

Contented people

We have seen our psalmist as a warrior and a patriot. Surely he is a painter, too. Verses 12–15 provide us with a wholly delightful picture. The boys are growing up to manhood—reproductive powers will soon appear. The girls are curvaceous and inviting. The crops are good. The sheep are lambing well. The cattle will soon be ready for the show—there is no cause for fear of miscarriage. It is an idyllic scene of a contented pastoral people. 'Happy are the people who are so blessed!'

Like other skilful writers, our psalmist keeps his punchline to the end—'Happy the people whose God is the Lord!' (v. 15b). Here is a people with a strong faith in God and a deep allegiance to him. They pursue the ordinary professions of ordinary people, but with an eye to God and a desire for his approval. As the people of God, the rhythm of their worship is regular and the word of God is their guide. Thus they keep at bay the forces which destroy a nation—their standards of conduct are the standards of God. Happy is such a nation—'whose God is the Lord'.

REFLECTION

Memento mori—*remember you must die.*

Are these words:

(a) a warning?
(b) a glad prospect (see 1 John 3:2)?
(c) both?

For a SPRING MORNING

There is scarcely a cloud in the sky of this psalm. No mention is made of the sinister side of life; no bringing of a charge against God because he seems to be doing nothing about human wickedness; no rage against tyrants; no complaints. Well, there is a cloud in verse 20b ('the wicked he will utterly destroy'), but it is only the size of a man's hand. The psalmist and the poet, Robert Browning, would seem to agree: 'God's in his heaven—all's right with the world!' It is the psalm for a spring morning, or for those rare moments when, say, at the end of a Bach cantata, one comes to earth again and whispers, 'If that be so, there must be goodness at the heart of the universe.' It's the psalm for a new day when the celebrant says, 'This is the day the Lord has made', and the congregation shouts back, 'We will rejoice and be glad in it.'

Look at the verbs—extol, bless (v. 1), praise (v. 2), commend, set forth (v. 4), speak of (v. 5), declare (v. 6), recite, sing (v. 7). Look at the description of God in his majesty—his compassion (v. 8), his might (v. 12), his faithfulness (v. 14), his nearness (v. 18), his care (vv. 19–20). Make your own list; this one is incomplete. But even as it stands, it gives the lie to the notion that the God of the Hebrew Scriptures is a stern, wrathful and remote figure.

Evangelistic task

'One generation will commend your works to the next and set forth your mighty deeds' (v. 4). This pinpoints the evangelistic task of the Church as one age leads on to another. 'We have a gospel to proclaim', to 'commend' to the upcoming generation, to pass on in its entirety, to interpret in terms that can be understood, to relate to new knowledge. The Church which is not alert to this task will perish in its tracks. One of the litmus tests of the vitality of the Church in any generation is its obedience to the divine commission: 'Go… to all nations and make them my disciples' (Matthew 28:19).

This verse (4) pinpoints also the liturgical task of the Church—the primary place of worship in its life and thought—'to set forth his most worthy praise,' as the 1662 Prayer Book puts it. Generation after generation, all over the world, in great cathedrals and under African trees, in humble kitchens and by the side of hospital sickbeds, the divine work goes on. I see worship as a vast river, a universal stream, into which each generation, each local church, each worshipping individual, makes its own contribution. Or, if you prefer a different picture, I see it as an eternal orchestra, making its praise heard in heaven. Into this ongoing music, I chip in. If, by reason, let us say, of extreme sickness, I am unable to pray or join in public worship, the music goes on and I need not worry. Or if my contribution is a bit flat or out of tune, it is subsumed into the music of the Church where Church triumphant and Church militant unite before the throne. My littleness matters little. My faithfulness in evangelism and in worship matters much.

LET US WORSHIP

We praise thee, O God: we acknowledge thee to be the Lord.

A HEART *for the* POOR

A few years ago, some Christians, when speaking about God, would refer to his 'bias towards the poor'—the phrase has faded a little since then. I was never very fond of it. I don't think my God is biased in any one direction. But I know what they meant. They were trying to say that God has a deep concern, frequently expressed in Scripture, for the underdog, and for this reason: that he is, in his very nature, a God of justice. To that view of God, the psalmist would certainly subscribe.

The God of his forebears is the God of creation, a God always true to his word (v. 6), a God of justice (v. 7). Then comes a list of those whose welfare is close to his heart—the oppressed, the hungry, the prisoners, the blind, the bowed down, the foreigner, the fatherless, the widow (vv. 7–9). This care for the underdog is a favourite theme of the prophets as well as of the psalmists, and it seems to have been a central concern in the teaching of Jesus himself. It is deeply significant that when Jesus preached his first sermon in the synagogue of his home town, he chose as his text a typical passage from Isaiah (Luke 4:16–20 and Isaiah 61:1–2a). He was the anointed (christed) one. The 'Christ' (or 'Messiah') was God's 'anointed', and he had been anointed to announce good news to the poor, to prisoners, to blind, to broken victims... Jesus shared his Father's passionate concern.

Any form of Christianity, any presentation of the Christian faith, which has not this at the heart of its gospel is a sham. The doctrine of the Incarnation, the Word enfleshed, is denuded of its meaning if its social relevance is not constantly made clear. This is God's world, and anything which spoils it—its earth, its air, its water—stands under the judgment of God. This is God's world, and anything which damages the welfare of its inhabitants—the health of the bodies and minds and opportunities for growth of its people—incurs his wrath. To join the Church is to join a Body dedicated to costly care. A Christian unconcerned with the ethical application of his or her faith is a contradiction in terms.

Here is a matter for repentance and for action.

LET US REPENT

Lord, you placed me in the world
to be its salt.
I was afraid of committing myself,
afraid of being stained by the world.
I did not want to hear what 'they' might say.
And my salt dissolved as if in water.
Forgive me, Father.

Lord, you placed me in the world
to be its light.
I was afraid of the shadows,
afraid of the poverty.
I did not want to know other people,
and my light slowly melted away.
Forgive me, Jesus.

Lord, you placed me in the world
to live in community.
Thus you taught me to love,
to share in life,
to struggle for bread and for justice,
your truth incarnate in my life.
So be it, Jesus.

Peggy M. de Coelho, Uruguay, in *Prayers Encircling the World* (SPCK)

LET US PRAY

Father, your world cries out for justice and mercy to the poor and
oppressed. We have no strength to speak out, to stand up for
justice to the poor. But you are our strength and your word is our
guide. Help us to do what is right. Help us to challenge the
structures of today that keep the poor in bondage to debt, while the
rich world profits. Help us to take action and proclaim a day of
freedom, through Jesus Christ our Lord.

SIMPLE ENJOYMENT

'Till you can sing and rejoice and delight in God, as misers do in gold, and kings in sceptres, you never enjoy the world.' The words are those of Thomas Traherne (c. 1636–74) from his *Centuries of Meditation*. The thought is close to that of the psalmist who wrote, 'Let Israel rejoice in their maker' (Psalm 149:2). God is to be enjoyed—do we believe that? Mother Julian did. She wrote, 'The simple enjoyment of our Lord is in itself a most blessed form of thanksgiving.' And again, 'God is our sure rock, and he shall be our whole joy…' How different is this idea of God from that image of him which all too many have—of a being who is rather sour-faced, ready to catch us out!

The other side of this golden coin is that God enjoys us. Our psalmist asserts that the Lord's 'pleasure is in those who fear him, who wait for his steadfast love' (v. 11). Listen to Mother Julian again: she pictures God as one 'who loves us and enjoys us… who is swift to clasp us to himself, for we are his joy and his delight, and he is our salvation and our life'. What a transforming concept of religion this picture gives us! It is a religion of mutual enjoyment—the creature enjoying the Creator and the Creator enjoying the creature. This is liberation indeed.

A positive picture

The picture of God which this psalmist gives us is a very positive one: he gathers in the scattered (v. 2); he heals the broken and the wounded (v. 3); he is a God of power and wisdom (v. 5) and of justice (v. 6); a God who cares for his creation (vv. 8, 9, 14–18). The beautiful imagery of verses 14–18 recognizes the Creator's continuing involvement in the creation, renewing and watering the earth, providing times and seasons, and 'the best of wheat in plenty'. This list of attributes reaches its climax in the last two verses: he is a God who 'reveals his word' (v. 19); that is to say, he discloses what is on his mind and heart. He is a God of revelation. Further, he has decided to make that revelation, uniquely, to Israel as to no other nation. If we want culture and philosophy, we may look to Greece. If we want law and direction in government, we may look to Rome. But if we want to see the mind and purpose of God for the welfare of humankind, we look to Israel—'He has not done this for other nations, nor were his decrees made known to them' (v. 20). It is a big claim; but it was through Israel that the Law was given and from Israel that the Messiah came. Jerusalem may well 'sing to the Lord'; Zion may well praise her God (v. 12).

LET US PRAISE

I love you, O Lord, you alone;
my refuge on whom I depend;
my maker, my saviour, my own,
my hope and my trust without end.

Christopher Idle (b. 1938)

PSALM 148

A Long Hallelujah

This psalm asks for nothing. It simply praises God. The writer pours out his heart in adoration to the Creator of the universe (vv. 1–6: heavens, angels, hosts, sun and moon, shining stars), and, coming nearer home, to the Creator of our earth with its infinite variety of ocean depths, the elements of fire and wind, the beauty of mountains and hills, of trees and animals, of humankind, of youth and age (vv. 7ff.). All are called on to 'praise the name of the Lord' (v. 13). The psalm is one long hallelujah, a cry of awe and wonder.

We are bidden to listen to the song of praise that creation sings, to join in the ongoing hymn of the universe. We are to become aware of our place in creation, of our relationship with the Creator, with all creation and all created beings. This will lead to a realization of our own littleness and yet to a realization of the uniqueness of our humanity. As the poem of George Herbert quaintly but pointedly put it:

> *Of all thy creation both in sea and land*
> *Only to man thou hast made known thy ways,*
> *And put the penne alone into his hand*
> *And made him Secretarie of thy praise.*

Ours is a God who delights in contrasts—night and day, contrasting colours in tree and field and garden, in colour of skin and variety of personality. God loves his creation: we should love it too, treasure it and respect it, enjoy it and revel in it. 'My God, how wonderful thou art!' the old hymn said. Yes, and how wonderful thy works as seen in the created order! How blind we are!

> *Earth's crammed with heaven,*
> *And every common bush afire with God;*
> *But only he who sees, takes off his shoes,*
> *The rest sit round it and pluck blackberries...*
> **(Elizabeth Barrett Browning, *Aurora Leigh*)**

To care for God's earth, the purity of its water and its air, the fruitfulness of its soil, is to engage in a religious act, for we are bound together with all the other parts of God's creation in a unity which awaits our discovery. There is a sacramental mystery uniting us with the earth, alive and life-giving.

PRAYER

We pray for God's forgiveness for our blindness to the beauty of his creation and our deafness to the song of praise that creation sings.

With Francis of Assisi we pray:

> *Most high, omnipotent, good Lord,*
> *To you be ceaseless praise outpoured*
> *And blessing without measure.*
> *Let every creature thankful be*
> *And serve in great humility.*

Praise *with* Dancing

On Sunday 19 July 1998, in Canterbury Cathedral, there was a great service to mark the opening of the Lambeth Conference, to which some eight hundred bishops and their spouses came. Those who were present at it and those who saw part of it on television may have been surprised that the service included some dancing. It was surprising, and it was also very beautiful. The young dancers, male and female, danced their way down the great central aisle, their white garments flowing like a tide, the splashes of colour round their waists contrasting with the purity of the abounding whiteness.

The placing of this dance within the liturgy was significant. It came immediately after the reading of the Gospel (a word which means 'good news'). As I watched it again on television, it seemed to me to be an exhibition of pure and uninhibited joy. The dancers seemed to be saying, 'If this to which we have just listened be true, we must give expression to our joy. It cannot be uttered in words. It must be expressed in action—through our bodies. Come on, let's dance, dance for joy, dance with abandon. Come on! Let's dance!' And dance they did.

Expressing our feelings

The psalmists knew about this. The man who wrote this psalm bids his readers praise God's 'name in the dance, and sing to him psalms with tambourine and lyre' (v. 3). The writer of Psalm 150 includes 'tambourines and dancing' among his list of calls for participants in joyful worship. These invitations raise the question as to why we, especially we British, are so slow to give outward expression to our religious feelings. Rather proudly we say, 'We do not wear our religion on our sleeves.' Quite so: we should not engage in a frothy emotionalism nor should we try to whip up a sentimental response to God's outgoing grace. But bodies are given to us to use for God's glory, and a sloppy slouch in church or a muttered participation in hymns of joyful praise does nothing to add to it.

Our psalmist bids us 'sing to the Lord a new song'. 'Why can't we have the good old hymns?' is a cry often heard. Why not, indeed? Some of them are almost as enduring as the gospel of which they tell (and some unutterably vacuous and inappropriate for modern use). But it is not a question of either the old or the new. For one of the most encouraging signs of the last two or three decades has been the production of new songs of praise, strong in wording, powerful in doctrine, and set to tunes musically attractive and worthy of the words to which they are set. Too easily we get into a rut, a groove; and a groove can be next to a grave. That is true of worship, as it is of many other things. 'Sing to the Lord a new song.'

A shadow is cast over the scene by the inclusion of verses 6b–9. As we have often seen, for the psalmists the picture is incomplete without the final vindication of God: for them, 'this is glory for all his loyal servants' (v. 9b). But it is hard for us to put it in the context of joyful, exuberant praise.

AN INVITATION

Come! Let us raise a joyful song to the Lord,
a shout of triumph to the rock of our salvation.
Let us come into his presence with thanksgiving
and sing psalms of triumph to him.
(Psalm 95:1–2)

SHOWING THANKSGIVING

This is the last psalm of the little group of six (it began with 145) which is concerned almost entirely with praise and thanksgiving. If Psalm 149 introduced us to dancing in worship, this psalm concentrates on music in worship. But not before the psalmist has taken one backward look at history, for it is in such acts of power that God manifests himself: verse 2 to any Jewish reader would speak of God's dramatic rescue of his people from the tyranny of Egypt. There God displayed 'his immeasurable greatness'. That was cause for endless thanksgiving.

Just how should that thanksgiving be shown? The psalmist fastens on the use of instrumental music, orchestral music, wind instruments, stringed instruments; he gives a lovely, noisy list! (vv. 3–5). But its climax—and indeed the climax of the psalter—is in verse 6. The best part of worship is personal, not instrumental. People are called on to use their lungs in praising the Lord. While they have breath in their bodies, they are to 'praise the Lord'.

We in the West are accustomed to the use of organ or piano in our services; more recently the accompaniment of orchestral instruments and of guitars is being used. We should also be open to what other countries have to teach us. Drums featured in the worship of the 1998 Lambeth Conference, and who of us who were present at the corresponding 1978 Conference will ever forget the offering of a steel band from the Caribbean? Rhythm and beat spoke of jubilation and abandon, and the great echoing vastness of Canterbury Cathedral took up the theme. (See also Psalm 33.)

Engaging in praise

Praising the Lord is not to be confined to cathedral and church services. All of us are called on to engage in such praise. But what does this mean to someone immersed in the necessity of keeping body and soul together, of running a business, of managing an unruly family, of facing another day in a long-drawn-out old age? How under these circumstances do we 'praise the Lord'? It may help us to practise the art of the upward glance and the quick under-the-breath utterance of just these words: 'Thank you, Lord.' Life is full of occasions which may

prompt this response to the goodness of God—a touch of colour un-
noticed before, the receipt of an unexpected letter, the kindly glance
of a friend, the helpfulness of a shop assistant, even the discipline of
pain which teaches patience and leads to the building of Christian
character. 'Thank you, Lord,' we say; and in saying it we add our tiny
bit to the Church's ongoing river of praise which constantly flows
before the throne of God.

LET US PRAISE

Almighty God, Father of all mercies...
We bless you for our creation, preservation,
and all the blessings of this life;
but above all for your immeasurable love
in the redemption of the world by our Lord Jesus Christ,
for the means of grace, and for the hope of glory...

From the General Thanksgiving, *Alternative Service Book 1980*

Let all things their creator bless,
And worship him in humbleness;
O praise him, alleluia!
Praise, praise the Father, praise the Son,
And praise the Spirit, Three in One;
O praise him, O praise him,
Alleluia, alleluia, alleluia!

Based on Francis of Assisi's *Canticle of the Sun*

EPILOGUE

As it was, as it is, and as it shall be
Evermore, God of grace, God in Trinity!
With the ebb, with the flow, ever it is so.
God of grace, O Trinity,
with the ebb and flow.

G.R.D. McLean, from *Poems of the Western Highlanders*

NOTES

NOTES

NOTES

NOTES